WHY ALL THESE DENOMINATIONS?

Why
All These
Denominations?

A Brief History of the Church in Britain

GILBERT KIRBY

KINGSWAY PUBLICATIONS
EASTBOURNE

Biblical quotations are from the
New International Version
© International Bible Society 1973, 1978, 1984

Front cover photos: Left – Howard Barlow
Top centre – The Telegraph Colour Library
Bottom centre and right – Mick Rock, Cephas Picture Library

British Library Cataloguing in Publication Data

Kirby, Gilbert W. (Gilbert Walter)
Why all these denominations?
1. Great Britain. Christian Church.
Denominations
I. Title
274.1

ISBN 0–86065–605–5

Printed in Great Britain for
Kingsway Publications Ltd
Lottbridge Drove, Eastbourne, E Sussex BN23 6NT by
Richard Clay Ltd, Bungay, Suffolk.
Typeset by Watermark, Hampermill Cottage,
Watford WD1 4PL.

To Gillian, David, Ruth and PJ
who with their partners and families
are a constant source of joy
to Connie and myself

Contents

Preface

My sole qualification for writing such a book as this lies in the
fact that my whole life has been cast in an interdenominational mould. My mother prior to marriage had been a
staunch Anglican, while my father came from non-conformist
stock. At the time I arrived on the scene they were worshipping at a Methodist church. Later, on moving to Bromley in
Kent, they joined a Congregational church, but I was sent to
an interdenominational bible class. As I grew up I chose to
worship fairly regularly at a local evangelical Anglican
church, although after leaving university I was ordained into
the Congregational ministry. With a pedigree like mine it is
not surprising that after two pastorates in Congregational
churches – at Halstead in Essex and Ashford in Middlesex – I
was called to serve as General Secretary to a society which had
its members drawn from all the denominations: the Evangelical Alliance.

After nearly ten years as General Secretary I was invited to
become Principal of the London Bible College – another
interdenominational body. During my period of service I also
served as honorary pastor of two different free churches –
Turners Hill in Sussex and Roxeth, Harrow, in Middlesex –
then subsequently acted as Moderator of two Baptist
churches, at Stanmore in Middlesex and Bushey in Hertfordshire. To complete the saga, my wife and I now find ourselves

worshipping at Northwood Hills Evangelical Church, which came into being as a Brethren assembly.

I do not advocate for everyone such a hybrid existence denominationally, but at least I can claim to have had some inside experience of most of the churches mentioned in this book. I can also testify to the fact that in my view no one denomination has a monopoly of the truth, nor of God's favour, but each has a valuable contribution to make to the body of Christ as a whole

Some of the material in this book appeared in print over twenty-five years ago. In completely revising it I have been impressed by the sweeping changes that have taken place in the intervening years. No denomination has remained as it was. The Church of England has settled for synodical government and in many cases adopted the Alternative Service Book in place of the Book of Common Prayer of 1662. Brethren assemblies now present themselves as 'evangelical churches', and some even have a full-time pastor. Both the Congregational Church and the Presbyterian Church of England have virtually disappeared to make way for the United Reformed Church. Services in many churches are unrecognisable compared to what they once were. There is greater freedom in worship and more congregational participation. New worship songs have become popular, sometimes at the expense of the older and much-loved hymns. In many churches the Authorised Version of the Bible has been replaced by the Good News Bible, the New International Version or the Revised Standard Version. And of course the whole church scene has changed dramatically in the last twenty-five years due to the emergence of the house church movement. I have therefore felt it appropriate to comment at greater length on this new challenge to the traditional churches.

In many parts of the country afternoon Sunday Schools have disappeared and churches have increasingly turned to family services in the morning. Single-sex youth movements have in most cases opened their doors to both sexes. The age-old barriers between clergy and laity have been broken down in an age when almost everyone is on Christian name terms.

What the future holds is hard to predict – hopefully spiritual revival in all its fullness! To quote a hymn of the past:

> Mercy drops round us are falling
> But for the showers we plead.

God is surely at work in his church and it can never be quite the same again.

Finally, I should like to acknowledge the painstaking work of two good friends, Doreen Bairstow and Lyn Simmons, who typed the manuscript for me in a remarkably short space of time. They did this at a time when they themselves were under particular pressure. I would also like to thank Marge Hance for her help and encouragement. Like the Apostle, I thank God for 'those women who have worked very hard in the Lord'; without their help my task would have been impossible.

GILBERT KIRBY

1

Roman Catholicism

The Book of Acts reveals how quickly Christianity spread throughout the civilised world. Within thirty years it had penetrated into Syria, Asia Minor, Greece and Rome. This same earnest commitment to evangelisation continued into the second and third centuries, often in the face of fierce opposition. Local churches were formed and visited by Christians from other localities. There was a pervading sense of oneness throughout the Christian community.

When or how Christianity first came to Britain is not known. It could have been introduced towards the end of the first century through a Roman soldier being posted to the country. It is generally supposed that Christianity was brought to Britain from Gaul, where in the south, in the districts of Lyons and Vienne on the Rhone, there were flourishing Christian churches as early as AD 177. We do know that early in the third century Tertullian, writing in North Africa, refers to 'territories in Britain, inaccessible to the Romans, having been won for Christ'. We also know of the martyrdom in the year 304 of a Roman officer, Alban. It is recorded that three bishops from Britain attended a Church Council at Arles in the year 314. It is highly likely that representatives from Britain were present at the Council of Nicaea in 325. Round about the year 450 the British missionary, Patrick, made his way to Ireland, and early in the sixth century David the Welsh missionary was active in Wales. We also have evidence that Columba, an Irish Christian who lived on the island of Iona, evangelised the country of the Picts north of the Grampians.

When Augustine came to Britain in 597 he found an organised church in existence. He was sent to Britain by Pope Gregory, Bishop of Rome. The Council of Chalcedon in 451 had agreed that the Bishop of Rome, Leo the Great, should be called 'pope' and that such a title should be used exclusively of him and of his successors. He strove to be recognised as Universal Bishop. The Church in the East, based on Constantinople, strongly repudiated such claims. Gregory the Great (Pope from 590 to 604) did much to increase the prestige of the See of Rome and renewed Leo's claim to universal supremacy. He claimed to be 'successor of Peter' and the 'Vicar of Christ on earth'. He taught that there was no salvation outside the one Catholic Church of which he was head.

By the beginning of the seventh century, teaching we associate today with the Roman Catholic Church was becoming widely acceptable – the idea that the Lord's Supper was itself a sacrifice and not merely a memorial of the death of Christ, the doctrine of purgatory, prayers to the saints, the adoration of Mary as the mother of God, auricular confession, together with increasing ritualism in church worship. Monasticism was also on the increase.

When Hildebrand became Pope in 1073 he claimed that as Vicar of Christ and representative of Peter he could give or take away empires and kingdoms, and he decreed that everyone on earth, from the emperor down to the humblest peasant, must acknowledge him. Priests were to be seen as a class apart and were required to remain celibate. He demanded that the secular head of the Holy Roman Empire should prostrate himself at his feet. Hildebrand conceived the idea of the crusades which were carried out unsuccessfully by those after him.

By the time of Pope Innocent III (1198–1216) the papacy had reached the height of its power. The Pope's political power extended throughout Christendom, and this situation continued until the days of Pope Boniface VIII (1294–1303) who claimed that 'for every human creature to be subject to the Roman pope is altogether necessary for salvation'.

There was, however, growing hostility to the papal claims on the part of national rulers. The papacy was weakened to such an extent that at one time there were two or three rival popes each claiming to be the only true occupant of 'Peter's chair'. Furthermore, there were a growing number of sects which protested against the corruption of the church, and even within the church itself there was disquiet.

John Wyclif, the great forerunner of the Reformation, declared that the only Head of the church is Christ and claimed many of the practices of the Church of Rome were unscriptural. The great Christian humanists such as Savonarola, John Colet and Erasmus, paved the way for the Reformation which began with Martin Luther in Germany and eventually came to England when King Henry VIII proclaimed himself to be the head of the Church in England in 1534. The Reformation continued under Edward VI, although the rule of Rome was temporarily re-established under Mary (1535–1558). Elizabeth I's reign saw the Act of Supremacy of 1559 which made the Queen Supreme Governor of the Church of England, and the Act of Uniformity which made it obligatory for all to join in public worship using the same order.

From that time on Britain has been regarded as a Protestant country, and there was little contact between the Church of England and the Church of Rome. As time went on a more tolerant attitude was discernible. In 1828 the Test and Corporation Acts were repealed and Roman Catholics were given permission to sit in Parliament. Leaders in the Oxford Tractarian Movement sought to prove the Church of England had unbroken continuity with the Catholic Church, and Roman Catholic ideas and practices were brought back. In October 1845 John Henry Newman, who had been a leader in the Oxford Movement, was formally received into the Roman

Church where he later became a cardinal.

On the whole the nineteenth century witnessed increased influence by the Roman Church. The Jesuit Order which had been suppressed in 1773 by Pope Clement XIV was revived under Pope Pius VII. The Jesuits were instrumental in getting the acceptance of the doctrine of the Immaculate Conception of the Virgin Mary (that she was born without original sin). At the Vatican Council of 1869–70 the doctrine of Papal Infallibility was decreed. This teaches that when the Roman pontiff, speaking 'ex cathedra', defines a doctrine regarding faith or morals, he is infallible by virtue of his supreme apostolic authority. There was a marked increase in the numerical strength of the Roman Church in Britain during the last century, partly accounted for by an influx of Irish immigrants. It was, however, left to the present century to witness dramatic changes in the Roman Catholic Church.

Pope John XXIII, elected in 1959, was responsible for convening the Second Vatican Council, and in so doing he ushered in a new era. His declared aim was to update the Church. Protestants were no longer to be dubbed as heretics or schismatics but were to be regarded as 'separated brethren'. Representatives from non-Roman churches were invited to attend the Second Vatican Council as observers. The cast-iron grip of the Curia was loosened. The use of Latin in the mass was no longer required, and Roman Catholics were encouraged to read the Bible for themselves. Catholic theologians like Hans Küng began to appeal more directly to the teaching of Scripture.

In spite of so many encouraging signs of change in the Roman Church there remains the underlying assumption that the ultimate goal is for the 'separated brethren' to return to the one fold. The essential conception of the Church as being the continuing presence of Christ, and its basic structure, are regarded as matters which cannot be discussed. Pope John XXIII for all his enlightened ideas declared, 'The focal centre of the entire visible unity of the Catholic Church is the Bishop of Rome.' The authority of the bishops 'cannot be exercised except with the consent of the Roman Pontiff'. It would seem the official position is that Rome is willing to change on secondary matters but on issues of dogma she remains as intractable as ever.

Nevertheless we would be wrong to minimise the changes which Vatican II brought about. Traditional teaching on transubstantiation has been modified. Sacrifice is no longer defined in terms of repetition but rather of re-presentation. Services are much simpler.

While Vatican II has been a major contributory factor in the changes taking place in the Roman Catholic Church in recent years, the charismatic movement has been even more influential. The Belgian Cardinal Suenens has been a prominent figure in the Catholic Renewal movement. 'What makes an authentic Christian?' he asks. 'A personal saving encounter with Jesus, the Lord, the one who baptises in the Holy Spirit,' he replies. 'Conversion, baptism, encounter with Jesus as Lord and Saviour, receiving the Holy Spirit, are all parts of a unique whole, a complex reality.'

Future visible unity, the Cardinal insists, must find its focus in the Spirit, for, he says, 'It is the Spirit who unites us in the acclamation "Jesus is Lord".'

Broadly speaking there are three kinds of Roman Catholics today: (1) those who have obviously been influenced by the charismatic movement, who lay a great emphasis on faith as a personal commitment and who are eager to follow the teaching of Scripture; (2) the 'liberals' who have been conditioned by modern rationalistic thought and who cast doubts on the infallibility of Scripture; and (3) the traditionalists who adhere strongly to the whole of credal Roman Catholicism and who are totally loyal to all Papal utterances. One thing is clear these days, Roman Catholics are not all alike. Some are becoming evangelical in outlook, others are not. Since Vatican II there has been a widespread movement away from traditional dogma.

For many Roman Catholics being baptised in the Spirit is tantamount to new birth. In many areas of the world Catholics and Protestants are finding reconciliation and peace, unity, love and joy under the sovereign, renewing work of the Holy Spirit. Nevertheless, we must face the fact that the Roman Church still sees herself as the infallible repository of divine truth with a priesthood tracing its succession back to the Apostle Peter and governed by popes who claim in literal fact to be his successors in unbroken line as Bishops of Rome, the divinely appointed Vicars of Christ upon earth.

While much has not changed, in certain areas the changes within the Roman Catholic Church have been dramatic. It is not unusual to find Catholic renewal fellowships, Bible study groups and prayer groups in Roman Catholic parishes, and also to hear the faithful singing identical worship songs to those being sung in many Protestant circles. Many churches are far less ornate than formerly. Yet this fact remains: that, in theory at least, Roman Catholics are committed to believing doctrines which are without scriptural foundation, such as the veneration of the Virgin Mary as the mother of God, invocation of the saints, purgatory, the sacrifice of the mass and the sacrament of penance.

The movement known as Catholic Pentecostalism emerged in 1966 among faculty members at Duquesne University, Pittsburgh, and within six years it claimed to have 50,000 members. In Britain, active members of the Roman Catholic Church total about 2,000,000. As with other denominations numbers have slowly been declining over recent years. Approximately one third of church members in England are at least nominally Roman Catholics.

In 1981 the Anglican-Roman Catholic International Convention (ARCIC) which first met in Windsor in 1970 presented its final report. Over the years delegates from the Church of England had worked alongside Roman Catholic delegates examining differing viewpoints on such matters as ordination and authority in the church, in the hope of finding a sufficient basis for taking further steps toward unity. Dr George Carey, Anglican Bishop of Bath and Wells, made this comment in a newspaper article:

The average Roman Catholic still wants to believe in the identity of the Catholic Church – that she still is doctrinally, ritually and morally the same the world over. Yet in his heart he knows that this is no longer the case and that Vatican II started something which has led to Rome's present identity crisis.

These recent changes in the Church of Rome have been variously interpreted by Protestants. On the one hand there are those who stoutly maintain that nothing has really changed; Rome still clings to her unscriptural dogmas. At the other extreme are those who loudly proclaim we share a common faith and the differences between us can be overcome. One quarter of all Roman Catholics, it is claimed, would say they are born again, and 20% insist that their only hope for heaven and eternal life is to be found through faith in Jesus Christ as Lord and Saviour. The fact is, like Protestants, some Roman Catholics have evangelical sympathies and some have not. Since Vatican II the position has changed and there are Catholics who are prepared to question some of the dogmas of their Church which would appear to have no foundation in Scripture. It is surely encouraging to find Roman Catholics increasingly open and ready to re-examine their traditions in the light of Scripture, and at the same time to know that the faithful are being actively encouraged to read their Bibles.

Traditionally Roman Catholicism has been most firmly established in certain areas of England such as London, Liverpool, Manchester, Leeds, Bradford and Birmingham, but the tendency in more recent years has meant that there are Roman Catholic communities spread throughout the country. Roman Catholicism is particularly strong in the Glasgow area where originally it was very much the church of the immigrant Irish. It is of course in Ireland where Roman Catholicism is at its strongest. In Eire it has a uniquely privileged status, but even in the Protestant north it represents a sizeable proportion of the population – in the region of 40%. Roman

Catholics are less numerous in Wales, proportionally, than in any other part of the British Isles.

On certain moral and ethical issues the Roman Catholic Church takes a particularly strong stand. Its stance on abortion is perfectly clear. The Pope's outright condemnation of artificial methods of contraception appears to have fallen on some deaf ears even within the ranks of the faithful. The Roman Church still requires from the non-Catholic partner in a mixed marriage a solemn undertaking that the children born of such a marriage shall be brought up within the Roman fold.

There are many aspects of Roman Catholicism which Protestants find off-putting, but there are clear signs that things are changing. Sadly the non-churchgoer hears references to Protestant and Roman Catholic antagonism in Northern Ireland and does not realise that often these terms are used politically rather than religiously. It is encouraging to know that barriers are being broken down in that country, not by political activists but by men and women truly filled by the Spirit of God – both Protestant and Roman Catholic.

2

The Church of England

No one knows who was first responsible for bringing the Christian gospel to our shores. Probably the earliest 'missionaries' were converted Roman soldiers, in which case the gospel may have been brought to Britain as early as the first century. We do know that Britain had been evangelised by the third century for in AD 314 a Church Council was held at Arles which was attended by three British bishops.

For a considerable time the form of Christianity here differed somewhat from that on the continent, but as time went on the power and influence of the Church of Rome became more and more marked. That church had departed considerably from the simplicity of the New Testament. After the Norman Conquest, English Christianity became even more 'Romanised' and the spiritual life of the country degenerated. From time to time men such as Wyclif and his Lollards stood up against the encroachment of Rome, but the years from AD 1000–1500 have been described as 'the Dark Ages' from the point of view of vital Christianity.

Near the end of the fifteenth century there was a remarkable revival of learning in Europe, and with it came a new spirit of inquiry. It soon dawned upon men that the Christianity they had always known was far removed from that of the New Testament. Tyndale translated the Scriptures into English, and this further paved the way for the enlightenment of the people.

During the reign of King Henry VIII the Church in England definitely broke with Rome. At this time Thomas Cranmer was Archbishop of Canterbury. Under the Supremacy Act, the king was declared to be 'Supreme Head of the Church of England' and the claims of the Roman Pontiff were repudiated.

At first there was little change within the church itself, although a growing number of men and women in the churches were eager to see reformation. In 1538 it was decreed that a copy of the Bible in English should be placed in every parish church and that the people should be encouraged to read it. It was during the reign of Henry's successor, Edward VI, that real spiritual progress was made. In 1549 the first English prayer book was published, and the effect of the Reformation was at last being felt in Britain.

In 1552 the second prayer book of Edward VI was published in which the Communion service was made more definitely Protestant in character. The words 'holy table' rather than 'altar' were used, and officiating clergy were expressly forbidden to use 'a vestment or cope'. Cranmer was largely responsible for this prayer book which remained basically the same for 400 years.

During the reign of Queen Mary there was a sharp reaction to the influence of the Reformation. The Pope was once more recognised as the head of the church in England and Protestants were persecuted for their faith. Men like Latimer, Ridley and Cranmer were burnt at the stake. 'Bloody Mary' was succeeded by Elizabeth I who, although she had no great love for the theology of the Reformers, finally broke with Rome and established herself as Supreme Governor of the church. The Thirty-nine Articles of Religion were agreed upon in 1562, and these provide an authoritative summary of the teaching of the Church of England.

A significant date in the history of the Church of England is 1662, when, during the reign of Charles II, the Act of Uniformity was passed which demanded the use of the prayer book in all church services. As a direct result of this enactment nearly 2,000 clergy resigned their livings and in many cases became the pastors of independent chapels.

Over the years the Church of England, in common with other branches of Christ's church, has seen many changes. It received a great new impetus at the time of the Evangelical Revival associated with such names as John and Charles Wesley, George Whitefield and the Countess of Huntingdon, all of whom were members of the established church. In the early nineteenth century the Clapham Sect, which included William Wilberforce, was instrumental in promoting social reform.

In the same century strong influences came from an altogether different quarter through the Oxford Tractarian Movement. The leaders of this movement – such men as John Henry Newman, John Keble and Edward Pusey – were keen to demonstrate that their church enjoyed unbroken continuity with the ancient Catholic Church, and they stressed the importance of tradition and 'apostolic succession'.

Many claim that the glory of the Church of England lies in its comprehensiveness. Certainly there are wide divergences of outlook between Anglo-Catholics with their insistence on tradition, evangelicals with their concern for the upholding of the Reformed faith, and the broad or central churchmen often associated with liberal views in theology and, as their name suggests, neither 'high' nor 'low' in churchmanship.

The late Dr Garbett, a former Archbishop of York, pointed out in his book *Church and State* a number of features that are peculiar to the Anglican Church:

> The Church has a unique relationship with the Sovereign. He must be a member of the Church of England and he promises at his coronation to protect its rights and privileges. He is crowned by the Archbishop of Canterbury. His chaplains in England are ordained clergy of the established church.

Furthermore the Archbishops of York and Canterbury and

the Bishops of London, Durham and Winchester, together with twenty-one other Bishops according to their seniority, have seats in the House of Lords. The State officially recognises the Church of England as the national church. The local vicar or rector has a recognised position in the community and has the responsibility for the spiritual welfare of all the people within his parish.

At the Reformation the Church retained the system of government known as *episcopacy* (from the Greek word *episkopos* meaning 'bishop'). The Archbishop of Canterbury is known as the Primate of All England. The country is divided into two 'provinces', Canterbury and York, and these are further sub-divided into 'dioceses', each under the supervision of a bishop. Archbishops and bishops are appointed by the Sovereign on the advice of the prime minister, although the prime minister works on the basis of advice from within the church. In each diocese there is a cathedral church to which is attached a dean and several prebendaries or canons. Together, referred to as the 'dean and chapter', they form the council of the bishop.

The local minister who is in full charge of a parish church may for historical reasons be known as either a rector or vicar, and he often has a curate (more properly called assistant curate) to assist him. When a candidate for the ministry is first ordained he serves as a 'deacon', and after about a year he is made a 'priest'. After serving as a curate in one or two parishes he is likely 'to be given a living' – ie, to become a local vicar.

A word ought to be said regarding the appointment of rectors or vicars to their charges or 'benefices'. The right to present or appoint a person to a benefice lies with the patron of the living. The patron may be the Crown, the bishop, a society, a private individual, or any other person or corporation recognised by law. In his parish the vicar is assisted by the Parochial Church Council, elected by parishioners whose names are on the electoral roll. The chief lay officers of the parish are the church wardens who are elected annually. In practice the elections usually take place in the context of or immediately prior to the annual parochial church meeting which may be attended by those whose names are on the electoral roll.

A few facts and figures will serve to give some idea of the strength of the Church of England today.

Although a large proportion of the population has been baptised in the Church of England, the total number who receive Holy Communion at Easter is under 1,750,000. The Church of England has approximately 16,000 churches and over 12,000 clergy.

In the Anglican Church infant baptism is the normal practice. It is stated in Article 27: 'Baptism is not only a sign of profession, and mark of difference whereby Christian men are discerned from others that be not christened, but it is also a sign of regeneration or new birth, whereby, as by an instrument they that receive baptism rightly are grafted into the Church....' Provision is also made for the baptism of those 'of riper years', who have not previously been baptised. In this case baptism is made conditional upon the repentance and faith of the candidate. When an infant is baptised, the child is regarded as being included in God's covenant of grace with its parents. Sureties or 'godparents' are required to guarantee that the infant shall be brought up 'in the nurture and admonition of the Lord'.

At the time of confirmation the spiritual privileges and blessings which are looked forward to at baptism are taken up as a conscious possession. The rite of confirmation affords the individual an opportunity for the confession of his discipleship and at the same time an occasion of union with others who are similarly related to God. This is the gateway to full membership in the Church of England and to all the benefits of church fellowship. The service is described as 'the laying-on of hands upon those that are baptised and come to years of discretion'. It is thus the complement of baptism, and it is intended only for those who accept the spiritual meaning of the rite.

As I wrote earlier, it is often said that the strength of the

Church of England lies in its comprehensiveness. In recent years, the evangelicals in particular have increased in strength. It would be true to say that a large section of the evangelical witness in England today is found within the established church. One of the explanations of this lies in the fact that there are a number of theological colleges training men for the Anglican ministry which are clearly committed to the evangelical point of view. Furthermore, there are Church of England missionary societies which are thoroughly evangelical in outlook. Evangelical Anglicans play a leading part in a number of interdenominational movements, such as the Universities and Colleges Christian Fellowship, the Scripture Union, the Keswick Convention, the Evangelical Alliance and many of the Christian youth movements. Societies such as the Church Pastoral Aid Society and Church Society play an important part in strengthening the evangelical position within the church itself. Much of the support for Dr Billy Graham in his crusades in this country came from members of the Church of England. It has been estimated that approximately one parish in ten is at least nominally evangelical in outlook, while a considerably higher proportion of ordination candidates are evangelicals. Evangelical clergy are, however, somewhat unevenly scattered throughout the country and are more numerous in the south than the north.

The Church of England has played an active part in the ecumenical movement, and the present Archbishop of Canterbury, like his predecessor, is President of the British Council of Churches. The whole question of intercommunion has a continuing place in discussions both within the church and with representatives of other denominations.

Reference has already been made to the growing vitality of the evangelical wing within the national church. In 1960, the Church of England Evangelical Council was formed. This, in turn, is part of an even larger body – the Evangelical Fellowship in the Anglican Communion – which seeks to link together Anglican Evangelicals throughout the world.

In April 1967 1,000 evangelicals in the Church of England

made their way to Keele University in Staffordshire for the first ever National Evangelical Congress. As John King remarked in his book *The Evangelicals*, Keele 'took the lid off contemporary evangelicalism'. One thing emerged most clearly – evangelicals in the Church of England had no intention of seceding from their denomination but rather of 'digging in their heels'. Another fact that became clear was that among evangelicals there was a serious 'generation gap' between the older 'die-hards' and the 'angry young men'. There were, of course, some very positive gains from Keele '67, although evangelicals in the free churches detected a degree of self-sufficiency in their Anglican counterparts, and accepted their protestations of friendship with a little scepticism.

Evangelical Anglicans at Keele made it clear that they were no longer prepared to see themselves as owing nothing of any importance to the historical church – they were part of it and intended to remain so. Furthermore, Keele committed evangelicals to ecumenical dialogue. In a 10,000-word statement, the delegates set out to restate the evangelical faith in clear, contemporary phraseology and to relate it to some of the major social and ecclesiastical issues of the day. Evangelical Anglicans pledged themselves to play a more active role in the life of the Church of England, and to be more concerned to make their voice heard in the secular world. In other words, the delegates turned their backs on both pietism and isolationism.

A new breed of evangelical Anglican had come on the scene – one which was prepared to face change and to assimilate new ideas rather than defend at all costs the status quo.

The theme at the next congress at Nottingham in 1977 was 'Obeying Christ in a Changing World'. Attention was focused on the Person of Christ, the church and modern society. The papers that were presented displayed an unusual combination of the conservative and the radical, the fixed and the free. Voices heard at Nottingham represented the thinking of a large segment of evangelical opinion within the established church.

The congress committed itself to work for the visible unity of the church and to continue in dialogue with Roman Catholics to that end. The subjects of evangelism and social responsibility were also much to the fore. Another matter touched on was the renewal of worship in the local church.

These two congresses demonstrated that changes were taking place within the evangelical wing of the Anglican Church. There was a new dynamism among the younger clergy. In a third such congress in 1988, with the title 'Celebration', evangelical Anglicans discussed where they stood in the midst of a divided church.

A most significant development took place in 1980 with the publication and subsequent authorisation of the Alternative Service Book. For nearly 400 years the Book of Common Prayer had remained the acknowledged norm for public worship throughout most of the Anglican Communion. The new book was intended not to supplant the old prayer book, but to offer an alternative form in more contemporary language. This move has been stoutly resisted by the die-hards, but generally welcomed by members of the church. In the preface to the new book, it is stated, 'New forms of worship do not erode the historical foundations of the church's faith, nor render respect for them any less appropriate than it was before.' One result of all this has been far greater variety in church services. There are presently many different forms of services in Anglican churches, although the church remains basically liturgical, and most services include such prayers as the General Confession and the reciting of the Apostles' Creed.

Probably the greatest impact on Anglican church life in recent years has come from the renewal or charismatic movement. The first Spiritual Renewal International Conference was held in Canterbury in 1978. The following year SOMA – Sharing Of Ministries Abroad – was formed with the express purpose of spreading the message of renewal to the wider world. Interestingly, the charismatic movement has not only influenced evangelicals in the Church of England, but has also received a warm welcome in some Anglo-Catholic circles and even among radicals.

There is a group known as Anglican Renewal Ministries which serves the cause of charismatic renewal in the Church. Renewal has brought a fresh emphasis on spiritual gifts and encouraged greater congregational participation in worship. It has also encouraged the concept of shared ministry so that in some parishes lay elders share with the vicar in the spiritual oversight of the parish.

An Anglican vicar once said to me that if you wanted to be sure that the order of service next week would be virtually the same as the previous week, you needed to attend the local Baptist church! His neighbouring parish church was very much caught up in the charismatic movement. In churches that have experienced renewal, there is a growing demand for spontaneity, participation and silence in worship. There is certainly much more lay participation in services than there used to be. In some churches, the liturgical content is minimal with an emphasis on singing and preaching such as would normally be associated with a free church service. As Josephine Bax comments in her book *The Good Wine*, 'The renewal has lifted us above our hobby-horses, with a real experience of living worship.'

All this has brought about considerable changes in the atmosphere of an Anglican church service. Often in the past, those entering the church building would be welcomed somewhat formally and be shown to a seat by a sidesman, and the period before the service began would be marked by complete silence. It is not uncommon today to walk into a church and be greeted warmly by two or three people and to find that everyone is chattering to one another in an animated fashion. On the walls of the church there may be colourful banners with such inscriptions as 'Jesus is King' or possibly a short verse of scripture. The surpliced choir has given place to a music group, complete with guitars. In the course of the service, a drama group may appear or there may be a contribution from a sacred dance group. After the service, coffee will no doubt be served and members of the congregation will be greeting one another warmly. Needless to say, there will be those who find all this rather embarrassing, just as many are not too happy about 'the peace' in the Communion service, where anything from a handshake to a hug is shared with those sitting near you. Not all will warm to this kind of physical expression of our sense of togetherness. It has never been more difficult to generalise about what happens at a typical Anglican church service!

For some years, the Church of England has adopted a system of synodical government. The General Synod with its house of both clergy and laity is effectively the parliament of the church. Topics discussed at Synod often find mention in the national press, especially if they are of a controversial nature.

The appointment of a bishop with doubts about the bodily resurrection of Christ occasioned questions about the degree of theological latitude the church should tolerate. Another debate has questioned whether or not the practice of Freemasonry is compatible with the Christian faith. Still another has discussed homosexuality in the church. The ordination of women issue has been temporarily side-stepped by the adoption of a compromise whereby women may now be ordained as 'deacons' but not as 'priests'. This means in effect that they cannot say the prayer for the consecration of the bread and wine at a Communion service.

There remain wide divergences of view within the Anglican Church. There are, on the one hand, staunch Protestants who view with suspicion any move which appears to be pointing in a Rome-ward direction, and on the other hand, there are extreme Anglo-Catholics who would welcome closer links with Rome. The publication of the report of ARCIC (the Anglican-Roman Catholic International Commission) in 1981 highlighted the degree of divergence there is in the Church of England. When all is said and done, however, the Church of England remains the national church and those who know no real church allegiance are usually content to regard themselves as 'C of E'. In such a privileged position the

Church of England has unique opportunities for evangelism, although it depends, under God, upon the keenness of the local vicar and the local church as to how far those opportunities are taken. Conservative evangelicals appear to be on course to dominate the Church of England by the end of the century, with at least 50% of ordinands sympathetic to that position. We have yet to see how this will make its impact on our increasingly secular society.

Critics of the Church of England point out that its leaders are masters of the art of compromise. They, on the one hand, reaffirm their faith in the historic creeds, but at the same time tolerate bishops who openly deny such fundamental truths as the Virgin Birth and the bodily resurrection of Christ. They permit the ordination of women but fail to grant them full ministerial status. They make strong pronouncements against the sin of homosexuality but take no action to purge the church of vicars who are known to be practising homosexuals. In other words there is all too often a 'fudging' of issues which the man in the pew finds perplexing. Maybe this is inevitable in a church which prides itself on being comprehensive.

Whereas the Church of England is episcopal in its form of church government, in Scotland the national church is Presbyterian. Episcopacy is nevertheless represented north of the border by the Scottish Episcopal Church. It has less than 40,000 members in total and just over 200 clergy assigned to nearly 300 churches. Like the Church of England it has its own General Synod, and it publishes a monthly magazine entitled *Newscan*. A number of missionaries serve overseas in various African countries, in the Indian subcontinent and in Latin America.

The Church of Ireland has some 150,000 church members with 300 ministers and about 450 churches. Generally speaking it appears outwardly to be strongly Protestant, although there is in it a decidedly high church tradition. The Church of Ireland was disestablished in 1870, and it has churches both in the North and in the Republic.

The Church in Wales, disestablished in 1920, has a number

of Anglo-Catholic parishes. It has some 136,000 members and about 700 clergy spread among 1,600 churches, and there is an Archbishop of Wales, chosen from among the Welsh diocesan bishops. The Church has made a determined effort to be fully identified with Welsh life and language.

3

The Presbyterians and the United Reformed Church

Most of the people who live in Scotland are Presbyterians and, of course, the Church of Scotland – 'the Kirk' – is Presbyterian in its form of church government. We must not, however, think of the Presbyterian Church as being exclusively or peculiarly Scottish. The membership of the Alliance of Reformed Churches throughout the world holding the Presbyterian order is drawn from many different countries, and it is conservatively estimated to number over 60,000,000.

The Church of Scotland is unique in that it enjoys national recognition and yet is entirely independent of State control. As the Queen's representative, the Lord High Commissioner attends the annual Assembly of the Church, but he does not address the Assembly except at the invitation of the moderator. The Church of Scotland claims some 900,000 communicant members, served by approximately 1,400 ministers.

There are several other Churches in Scotland which are Presbyterian in polity, the largest being the Free Church of Scotland with probably 14,000 members and adherents, and the United Free Church of Scotland with a smaller number. In England the Presbyterian Church was relatively small, but in 1972 it joined up with the Congregational Church in England and Wales to form the United Reformed Church with a total membership of about 135,000. The figure for Wales is about

77,000, and the membership in Ireland is nearly 250,000.

It has been said with justification that although the Reformation came to Scotland somewhat later than in some other countries, it was in fact more thorough there than anywhere else for it touched the very heart of the nation and had repercussions throughout the whole land. In Scotland the Reformation leaders, of which John Knox was the most notable, were from the very outset determined to establish an ecclesiastical polity which they believed to be founded directly on the teaching of the New Testament. Indeed, it was said of John Knox that while 'other men sawed the branches of the papacy, this man laid his axe to the trunk of the tree'.

In England the Presbyterians represented one wing of the Puritan movement. It was Thomas Cartwright, Professor of Divinity at Cambridge University, who, in his lectures on the Acts of the Apostles, first demanded publicly the remodelling of the polity of the Church of England in accordance with that of the primitive church. Cartwright has been described as 'the father of English Presbyterianism'.

The Presbyterians were profoundly dissatisfied with the English Church Settlement made by Queen Elizabeth I, but they endeavoured to bring about its reform by constitutional means. They sought to introduce their ecclesiastical systems within the framework of the established church. Movement along these lines was particularly strong in East Anglia and in parts of the Midlands. Ministers who were Presbyterian in sympathy submitted themselves to ordination by a bishop, but at the same time they offered themselves for approval and election by the local congregation before accepting a benefice, and they preferred to call themselves 'pastors' rather than vicars or rectors. In contrast to the radical movement led by Browne and his Separatists, with their watchword 'Reformation without tarrying for any', the Presbyterians adopted the policy of 'tarrying for the magistrate'.

Nevertheless, men like Cartwright were outspoken in their views regarding the Church and its worship. Cartwright affirmed that the Church was entitled to regulate its doctrine, polity and worship by the Word of God without restriction by the State; that the head of the Commonwealth was only a member of the church, not its governor; and that episcopacy as it was then known in England was purely a human growth.

John Knox, in the course of a five-year stay in England – during which time he was one of the Court Chaplains – inveighed against kneeling at the Lord's Table, since he interpreted this as constituting a recognition of the sacerdotal claim that the bread and wine were turned into the very body and blood of the Lord. While Cranmer and Ridley were prepared to accept kneeling as 'a seemly posture', Knox, with typical forthrightness, regarded it as a dangerous compromise with superstition.

During the reign of Charles I civil war broke out in England, and in 1649 the Commonwealth was set up. It was then that Presbyterianism really came into its own in England. The Westminster Confession of Faith – which had been officially adopted in Scotland in 1647 – replaced the Thirty-nine Articles, and a Presbyterian 'Directory of Public Worship' was substituted for the Book of Common Prayer. The Longer and Shorter Catechisms were brought into use for the purpose of religious instruction, and a metrical version of the Psalms was approved. Parliament was largely Presbyterian in outlook. Unfortunately, however, the Presbyterians, now that they were in control of the situation, were somewhat unimaginative and lacked the spirit of toleration. The new church was not popular. The observance of Christmas Day and other religious festivals was abolished. Civil marriage was substituted for a religious service. With the fall of the Cromwellian regime came the restoration of the monarchy and, within a few short years, the Act of Uniformity in 1662.

Many of the clergy who left their livings on St Bartholomew's Day in 1662 were Presbyterians who, during the Commonwealth, had secured parishes. A similar series of ejections in Scotland deprived more than 300 ministers of their parishes 'for conscience' sake'. Various attempts were made in the succeeding years to bring back the Presbyterians and even the Independents into a comprehensive church, but these were unsuccessful. Unfortunately, in the succeeding century the influence of Arian (or Unitarian) teaching was strongly felt in some Presbyterian circles in England, and with it came a loss of evangelical power and effectiveness.

In Scotland, the eighteenth century has been described as 'the Dark Age of the Scottish church'. Nevertheless, the Evangelical Revival which brought renewed spiritual life to England also had a profound effect across the border. Prior to that, religious life in Scotland, as in England, had certainly sunk to a low ebb. There were secessions from the Church in both 1733 and 1761, and 1843 witnessed the Disruption when no less than 478 ministers left the Church of Scotland and formed the 'Free Church of Scotland' on grounds of conscience, believing that the spiritual freedom of the church was being impaired.

In Wales, the Presbyterian Church also played a significant part. Strangely enough, however, it owes its origin to the eighteenth-century revival associated with the Wesleys and with George Whitefield, rather than directly to the Reformation, and it is usually known there as Calvinistic Methodism. At first Calvinistic Methodists were loth to part company with the Anglican Church and it was not until 1811 that the final step of separation was taken. This Church is Presbyterian in government and possesses a confession of faith very similar to the Westminster Confession. In 1904 the Welsh Revival, associated with the name of Evan Roberts, had its beginning in a Calvinistic Methodist Chapel.

The Presbyterian Church has extensive missionary interests overseas. In the case of the Church of Scotland, work is carried on in India and Pakistan, in Nepal and in various parts of Africa, in Israel and in the West Indies; while the Presbyterian Church of England had missionaries in Taiwan, Malaya, Bengal and East Pakistan. In 1977 it became part of the Council for World Mission. The Free Church of Scotland is responsible for work in South Africa, Peru and India.

What is the doctrinal and ecclesiastical emphasis of Presbyterianism? Traditionally, Presbyterianism looks to John Calvin as its founder and mentor. From Calvin Presbyterians learnt both their doctrine and their church polity. Historically, such emphases as election and predestination, total depravity and the final perseverance of the saints, are inherent in Presbyterian teaching. The basic emphasis is on the absolute Sovereignty of God. The Westminster Confession of Faith, which sums up these doctrines, remains the symbol of Presbyterian teaching throughout the English-speaking world. It has been described as 'the finest fruit of reformed theology'.

Presbyterianism owes not only its theological emphases to Calvin, but also its form of church government. The polity which Calvin devised and established in Geneva over 400 years ago is basically that which is followed by many thousands of Presbyterian churches throughout the world today. Presbyterians would say, of course, that Calvin 'rediscovered' Presbyterianism, believing that the earliest Christian churches were governed on similar lines. It has often been pointed out that in the early church 'presbyters' are far more frequently referred to as church officers than are bishops. Furthermore, it is claimed that in the early church a 'bishop' was synonymous with an 'elder' or 'presbyter'. The Greek *presbuteros,* meaning 'elder', has of course given the denomination its name.

In the local church responsibility for oversight is vested in the elders, known as the Kirk Session. The elders assist in various ways in running the church, arranging meetings, admitting new members, and supervising weekday activities of the church. They share with the minister in the pastoral work of visitation. All the elders are elected by the people of the church and are solemnly ordained to their office. The result of this is that very often Presbyterian elders take their office more seriously than is sometimes the case with their counterparts in some of the free churches. There are also deacons, sometimes known as managers, whose primary responsibility is the church fabric and financial matters. All elders are also deacons.

The most important unit of government is the presbytery, which unites the churches of a district and exercises a certain supervision of and control over them. The presbytery is made up of all the ministers in the district and one ruling elder for each minister. The minister is not a member of the local church but is a member of the presbytery. He is held responsible to and can only be removed by his presbytery or by a superior court. The presbytery examines, licences and ordains candidates for the ministry, installs them in churches and permits them (or does not permit them, as the case may be) to change churches. Above the presbytery is the Synod, which must include at least three presbyteries and usually covers the churches of a considerable area. The Synod usually meets once a year and deals with matters that have been raised by the presbyteries. The highest executive, legislative and judicial authority in the Presbyterian Church is the General Assembly. This also meets annually. Its decisions are final and binding on the whole church.

Looking out upon the scene today, certainly as far as England is concerned, it is hard to realise that there was a time when Presbyterianism was the strongest and largest body of Protestant dissent. In the eyes of many, Presbyterianism has always been 'the Scottish church', although it is not by any means true that the membership of the average English Presbyterian church was made up entirely of Scottish exiles. There were areas where the Presbyterian church served as the only local free church.

In 1876 the World Presbyterian Alliance came into being. This body meets every four years and links together most of the Presbyterian or Reformed churches throughout the world. Presbyterians have also been active in the ecumenical movement at all levels, and for some years conversations have been going on regarding Anglican-Presbyterian relations between the Church of Scotland and the Church of England.

As far as Scotland is concerned the Presbyterian Church was weakened by secessions in the eighteenth century and

more especially by the Disruption in 1843 when nearly a third
of its ministers and members left the establishment to form
the Free Church. The nineteenth and the present century
have witnessed a growing movement in the direction of
reuniting the different Presbyterian churches in Scotland, but
with each union a remnant remained outside. At the present
time probably 97% of Scottish Presbyterians are in fact linked
with the Church of Scotland.

What of worship in the average Presbyterian church? There
is no required order or liturgy but the local congregation is
free to adopt a liturgy if the majority so desire. There is an
official Book of Common Order which is used in many
churches. Great emphasis is placed upon the necessity of the
service being orderly and dignified. The Presbyterian minister
normally wears a cassock and gown with preaching bands
when he is conducting the service of worship. Regular use is
made of the metrical psalms. The demands made upon the
candidate for the ministry are exacting and much emphasis is
placed upon the need for good academic standards. The
whole ethos of Presbyterian worship is intellectual rather than
emotional, and to some nonconformists it would appear to be
somewhat cold and formal.

The two sacraments of baptism and the Lord's Supper are
observed in Presbyterian churches. The usual mode of baptism – 'a sign and seal of the covenant of grace' – is by sprinkling, and infant baptism is normally practised. Great emphasis
is placed upon the solemnity of the Lord's Supper, although
the local church determines how often and under what
circumstances it shall be observed. In the Church of Scotland
the Lord's Table is generally open to members of any branch
of the Christian church, but this is not so with all Presbyterians.

There is a practice among some churches, especially with
the congregations of the Free Church of Scotland in the High-
lands and the Hebrides, of 'fencing the Table'. It is a pre-
Communion convocation, usually held on the Friday or Saturday prior, and is intended to prepare the communicants for

the Lord's Supper on the Sunday.

A visiting minister is often called and entrusted with the solemn responsibility of 'fencing the Table', dealing with such scriptures as 'Therefore, whoever eats the bread or drinks the cup of the Lord in an unworthy manner will be guilty of sinning against the body and blood of the Lord' (1 Cor 11:27). On such occasions large numbers of people gather. Sometimes the visiting minister is so forthright in his preaching that comparatively few of those attending feel able to come forward to the communion table when the invitation is given on the Sunday.

Undoubtedly one of the greatest contributions of Presbyteriansim to the church has been its concern for expository preaching, its traditional emphasis upon the sovereign grace of God, and its stress upon the importance of church order. Theologically there are considerable differences within the Presbyterian family, ranging from extreme liberalism to ultra-fundamentalism. Generally speaking, there has been an increasing emphasis on evangelism in recent years. This found expression, for example, in the 'Tell Scotland' movement in connection with which training schools for both ministers and laymen were organised and numerous visitation campaigns held. Evangelical influence in the Church of Scotland is growing particularly with younger men in the ministry.

In Northern Ireland, the Evangelical Presbyterian Church of Northern Ireland left the main body in 1926 and has some 800 members; while Dr Ian Paisley's Free Presbyterians number some 11,000.

The Presbyterian Church of Wales has about 77,000 members, and there are about 62,000 in the Union of Welsh Independents.

Historically and theologically, Presbyterianism can claim a fine heritage, but this church, in common with all the churches, needs the breath of a heaven-sent revival which will bring new life and vitality to its members as well as quickening their evangelistic zeal.

The United Reformed Church, which came into being

in 1972 through the union of the Presbyterian Church of England and the Congregational Church, was further strengthened in 1981 by the addition of the Reformed Association of Churches of Christ, known in the USA as 'Disciples of Christ'. Within the URC there are considerable tensions between those who come from a liberal tradition theologically and those who accept the supreme authority and entire trustworthiness of the Bible as the word of God. As with most groups there are also differences between those who cherish more traditional forms of worship and those who prefer a freer style. Within the denomination the ginger group known as GEAR – the Group for Evangelism and Renewal – exerts an increasing influence. The URC makes play of the fact that as a denomination it is committed to taking 'wherever possible and with all speed, further steps towards the unity of all God's people'.

As far as numbers are concerned the United Reformed Church has some 130,000 members served by over 1,000 ministers. England and Wales are divided into twelve different provinces and they in turn are subdivided into districts. A moderator is appointed to give spiritual oversight to each of the districts.

In Scottish Presbyterianism, as well as in the United Reformed Church, great emphasis is placed on the academic qualifications required for the ministry. The result is that many congregations tend to have a cerebral approach to their faith, and there is a noticeable lack of exuberance in church life. This may explain how it is that, generally speaking, the renewal movement has made less impact on Presbyterian churches than on certain others.

4

Congregationalism

Although the year 1662 is of special significance in connection with the beginnings of nonconformity in Britain, it has always been a matter of debate as to just when and where the English free churches had their origin. The nineteenth-century historian, Skeats, claimed that John Hooper, Bishop of Gloucester in the reign of Edward VI, was the first nonconformist. 'It was Hooper's voice,' he said, 'that first publicly proclaimed the principles of religious freedom; he stood alone among English Protestants of his age in denying the right of the State to interfere with religion.' Some would claim that the origin of nonconformity is traceable back to the original Act of Uniformity, by which Edward VI in 1549 sought to enforce the use of the first English prayer book.

Dr R W Dale claims that 'the first regularly constituted English Congregational church of which any record and tradition remains was the church of which Richard Fitz was pastor'. This he identifies with a group arrested at Plumbers' Hall, London, on 19 June, 1567. Certainly the Plumbers' Hall Company were Puritans, but it is debatable whether they were actually Separatists. The title Puritan was first given in 1569 to certain clergymen in the Church of England who wanted to see their church more drastically purged of the influence of Rome. Later the name was applied more generally to 'all who were devout and serious in a holy life'.

The Puritans themselves were sharply divided over the issue of church government. The right wing party were quite content to remain in the established church and to accept the principle of episcopacy. A second party aimed at substituting a Presbyterian form of church government for episcopacy, while a third group, later known as Independents, were the out-and-out dissenters, as much opposed to Presbyterianism as to episcopacy. Their strong point was that 'each church has its right to elect its own officers, manage its own affairs, and to stand independent of, and irresponsible to all authority, saving that of the supreme and divine Head of the Church, the Lord Jesus Christ.' While it is true that the Baptist, Congregational and Presbyterian churches all owe their origin to the Reformation, the Baptists and Congregationalists are the modern counterpart of the early Independents or Separatists. In this chapter I shall deal particularly with those who are now known as Congregationalists.

Robert Browne is often regarded as the real founder of English Congregationalism. He, perhaps more than anyone else, kindled the reforming passion of the earliest nonconformists in England. For two or three centuries those who held to his doctrine of the church were known as Brownists. At Cambridge University he developed an ardent zeal for spiritual reformation in the church. He later attracted a great deal of attention by his forthright preaching in which he frequently attacked the Church of England and her episcopal form of church government. He stressed what he called the New Testament doctrine of 'the gathered church'. In about the year 1580 he called together a small company in Norwich and led them 'to join themselves to the Lord in one covenant and fellowship together, and to keep and seek agreement under his laws and government.'

During a time of exile in Holland, Browne wrote his famous pamphlet entitled *Reformation without tarrying for any*. This title probably sums up better than anything else Browne's attitude. His great contention was that the Church of Christ must be composed solely of men who by faith are truly Christ's disciples. It was not enough for a man merely to submit to the outward jurisdiction of the church. Furthermore, Browne contended strongly for the church to be entirely independent of the State. 'The church,' he held, 'is subject neither to bishops nor magistrates.' Ordination to preach is not in the hands of the elders merely, but of the whole membership. He urged Christian ministers not to wait for the civil power or the ecclesiastical authorities to bring about a Reformation, but to begin it themselves where they were with no authority other than that of Christ himself. Some would claim that Browne's Congregationalism represented the purest expression of Protestantism. There can be no question but that Browne's influence has been far-reaching on both the English and American way of life. Men like Browne laid foundations on which their successors were later to build.

The teaching of the Separatists found particular acceptance in East Anglia. It was there that the earliest Independent churches came into being. Many of these early Independents were put to death, and others were driven abroad in exile.

It was in 1620 that the *Mayflower* sailed from Plymouth to New England with a group of men, their wives and their families, determined to seek religious freedom in the New World because they despaired of ever finding liberty of conscience in their own land.

The closing years of James I's reign saw increased persecution, and his successor, Charles I, was strongly anti-Puritan. However, when civil war broke out in 1642, England swung over to Puritanism. During the Protectorate of Oliver Cromwell, Presbyterians, Congregationalists, Baptists and Episcopalians all occupied pulpits within parish churches. In some cases two congregations might be worshipping in different parts of a large church or cathedral at the same time. Congregational churches had their home in Westminster Abbey and Exeter Cathedral. The use of the Book of Common Prayer was forbidden. Under Cromwell, John Owen – a Congregational minister who was a man of great learning – became vice-chancellor of Oxford University.

The religious life of England during these years was in

strange confusion. It has to be confesssed that in their new-found rise to power some of the early Independents lost their truly spiritual emphasis. There was increasing tension between the Presbyterian and Separatist elements. The Presbyterians aimed at a uniform system of doctrine and practice enforced and protected by civil power. Independents, or Separatists, stood for liberty of conscience and pleaded for the liberty and autonomy of the local church. The faith and beliefs of the Independents were expressed in the Savoy Declaration of 1658, just as the Westminster Confession issued a few years earlier had expressed the doctrinal position of the Presbyterians.

After Cromwell's death, in the reign of Charles II, the Act of Uniformity was passed in 1662 whereby every beneficed clergyman was required to give his assent before August 24, to all and everything contained in the Book of Common Prayer, and to declare at the same time that it was not lawful upon any pretence whatsoever to take up arms against the king. Henceforth no ordination except at the hands of a bishop was to be recognised. The outcome of this act was that some 2,000 clergy left their livings, facing great hardship as a result. Up to 1662 many had cherished the ideal of a 'national' church comprehensive enough to embrace Episcopalians, Presbyterians and Independents, but that dream was now shattered and modern nonconformity was born. Many outstanding men left the Church of England at that time, including Richard Baxter and John Owen. Separatism spread rapidly, and in the last twelve years of the seventeenth century 2,418 Dissenters' meeting-houses were officially licensed for public worship. Independency grew chiefly among the middle and lower classes and seemed to thrive on persecution. The seventeenth century brought to light some honoured names amongst the nonconformists, including Milton, Cromwell, Baxter, Fox and Bunyan.

Generally speaking the eighteenth century may be described as the 'quiet time' of nonconformity. Doctrinal uncertainties arose and some churches passed through a phase of unitarianism. The names of two great Independents of this period do, however, deserve a mention – the hymn-writers Isaac Watts and Philip Doddridge. By the time of his death in 1748 Watts had become something of a national figure. His hymns have since found their way into the hymn-books of every Protestant church.

From a spiritual point of view the situation in the country generally was desperate immediately prior to the evangelical revival. Certainly the nonconformist churches no less than the established church needed the new life that came with the preaching of Wesley and Whitefield. By the 1820s the number of nonconformists had greatly increased. In all denominations there were signs of vigorous and expanding life. Trevelyan the historian says, 'The ultimate consequence of the revival was that nonconformists rose from about a twentieth of the church-goers to something near a half.'

Congregationalists found many of their old meeting houses full once more, and in all parts of the country there was an era of chapel building. New colleges were founded for the training of nonconformist ministers. In 1831 the Congregational Union was formed with the primary objective of 'promoting evangelical religion in connection with the Congregational denomination'. During the Victorian era the official status of nonconformity changed greatly. Universities were opened to nonconformists, and various other disabilities were removed. There was an awakening of the social conscience and a deepening concern for missionary work overseas. The Victorian age is often described as the 'golden era of noncon-formity'.

It was of course also during the nineteenth century that biblical criticism came into its own, and many of the noncon-formists, particularly the Congregationalists, were quick to accept what were then called 'the assured results of higher criticism'. The result in many cases was a departure from the evangelical faith, the full effect of which was to be felt in the twentieth century. D W Brogan in his book *The English People* says:

It is probable that nonconformity reached its height of political power, was most representative of the temper of the English people, round the beginning of this century ... but in the generation that has passed since the great Liberal landslide of 1906, one of the greatest changes in the English religious and social landscape has been the decline of nonconformity.

It is probably true that the Congregational churches more than any of the other free churches have lost ground during this present century, with the result that, with certain outstanding exceptions, the denomination became made up of relatively small churches.

The church meeting, of course, stands at the very heart of Congregational polity. It is this body which is responsible for inviting the minister and for formulating the policy of the church. The body of deacons is elected by the church members to act as a kind of executive committee, although the ultimate authority remains vested in the church meeting itself. After the Second World War, however, there was an increasing measure of centralisation within the denomination.

Membership in a Congregational Church is on the basis of acceptance of Jesus Christ as Saviour and Lord. He alone is regarded as Head of the Church. No credal tests are imposed upon those who join the church, but emphasis is placed on the responsibility of every member for the well-being and witness of the church. The names of those who are candidates for membership are brought before the diaconate, church membership classes are held, and, on the recommendation of the diaconate, the name of the candidate is then brought to the church meeting for acceptance. The 'right hand of fellowship' is given at the next Communion Service.

A Congregational church may best be described as a 'covenanted Christian fellowship'. Men and women who are themselves in covenant with God covenant together that as a church they will live in obedience to his will under the guidance of the Holy Spirit. Worship in a Congregational church is conducted on much the same lines as in any other free church. Congregationalism recognises two forms of baptism. The usual form is the baptism of infants and this takes place during the course of or at the end of a normal service of worship. Recognition is also given to the fact that the same sacrament may be administered to older people who are seeking baptism on profession of faith.

Congregational churches claim to be churches of the Holy Spirit, and their claim is that they are not 'enslaved by tradition or bound by customary forms'.

In 1966 the Congregational Union of England and Wales voted to become the Congregational Church in England and Wales, and this in turn was a prelude to the union with the Presbyterian Church of England in 1972 to form the United Reformed Church.

Congregationalism, however, refused to disappear, and the union in fact spawned two on-going Congregational bodies – the Congregational Federation and the Evangelical Fellowship of Congregational Churches. The Federation has its headquarters in Nottingham and has over 10,000 members, over 100 of whom are ministers. It is soundly established and widely respected. The Federation's constitution guarantees to each church its scriptural right to be independent. It claims to stand in and to continue the tradition of the original Congregational Union of 1831. Theologically its ministers represent varied views as to the authority of Scripture, and as a body it is committed to ecumenism.

In contrast, the Evangelical Fellowship of Congregational Churches has a strong basis of faith to which its members adhere. It is in membership with the British Evangelical Council rather than the British Council of Churches, but like the Federation it is committed to preserving the congregational way as far as church government is concerned. It consists of some 6,500 members.

As a denomination Congregationalism had been in sad decline for a number of years, and many would feel that this has been due in no small measure to the liberal theology which has infiltrated the denomination. There have always been, however, strong Congregational churches such as Westminster Chapel in London which have been great preaching centres and where there has been sound Bible-based teaching. The Evangelical Fellowship of Congregational Churches seeks to uphold that tradition.

5

The Baptists

It was early in the seventeenth century that Baptists were first seen in England as an organised body. On the continent of Europe there had been earnest Christians in the sixteenth century who were known as Anabaptists, (*ana* = again), because they rebaptised those who had already been baptised as infants. It is reckoned that there were nearly 300 Baptist churches founded in England and Wales by 1660.

In 1611 Thomas Helwys, an exile in Holland, led back from Amsterdam a separatist group who formed themselves into a Baptist church in London. Helwys and his followers insisted that the rite of baptism must be reserved for true believers and that the scriptural mode was total immersion, rather than affusion (pouring). The successors of Helwys and his friends became known as General Baptists. For the most part they believed in free will and were Arminian in theology. They adopted a form of church government somewhat akin to Presbyterianism. In contrast to these were other groups who later became known as Particular Baptists. They believed that the atonement was 'particular' – that is, restricted to those elected by God for salvation. They originated from a section belonging to a Calvinistic Separatist Church in London which, in 1633, broke away and adopted the practice of believers' baptism. They continued to be strongly Calvinistic in theology and adopted a form of church government based on the principle of independency. In later years some of the Particular Baptists linked up with the General Baptists, although to this day there is a distinct denomination of considerable strength hitherto known as Strict and Particular Baptists.

In the early years Baptists were subjected to particularly fierce persecution, especially at the time of the Restoration in 1660. From the outset they have been champions of religious liberty, and in many cases they have shown a radical approach to politics. Of all the different branches of nonconformity Baptists are probably the most suspicious of ecclesiasticism, and they have been the most ardent devotees of independency as far as church polity is concerned. Nevertheless there has been in existence since 1812 the Baptist Union of Great Britain and Ireland which links together in fellowship nearly 2,000 churches with over 150,000 members. Some Baptist churches, however, prefer to remain in complete independence and are not linked with the Union. A later chapter will deal with independent evangelical churches which, though in most cases Baptist in principle, are not members of the Union. The Baptist Union has divided the country into areas, and over these areas are appointed General Superintendents. These men act in a purely advisory capacity to the churches in their respective areas. The Baptist Union is in turn affiliated to the Baptist World Alliance – formed in 1905 – which is a worldwide fellowship of some 24,000,000 Baptists.

Obviously the feature that is of most interest to those who are not Baptists is the practice of baptism by immersion, or, to give it its correct designation, believers' baptism. Baptists insist that the only right and proper candidates for the ordinance are those who have already exercised faith, and they further maintain, appealing to such New Testament scriptures as Acts 8:36–39, that the proper mode of baptism is by immersion rather than by pouring or sprinkling water on the candidate. They stress the symbolism of the rite, as set forth by the Apostle Paul in the Epistle to the Romans (chapter 6, verse 4), where baptism is regarded as portraying death and burial to sin and resurrection to newness of life.

In warmer climes, of course, baptism by immersion can conveniently be carried out in the open air, in a river or in the sea, but in Britain and in other countries where this is scarcely possible special baptistries are constructed. These are usually located under the floor of the communion platform, in front of or beside the pulpit. The candidate descends down steps into the baptistry where he is met by the minister, or whoever is doing the baptising. He guides the candidate to the centre of the baptistry and asks him to make public profession of his personal faith in the Lord Jesus Christ. On receiving an affirmative answer, the baptism proceeds. The candidate is momentarily completely submerged and then lifted up from the waters of baptism, guided to the steps, and conducted to one of the vestries.

In general matters of church doctrine Baptists share the same principles and practices as other Free churches. For them the Bible is the ultimate rule of faith and practice, and church government follows the rule of independency, each local church being a self-governing body. Strong emphasis is laid on the doctrine of the priesthood of all believers. The local congregation chooses its own pastor, elects its own officers and administers its own affairs. Ordination normally takes place when a man has satisfactorily completed his college course and has been called to the pastorate of a local church. The ordination service may be presided over by the college principal or Area Superintendent, and the act of ordination involves the laying on of hands by representative ministers and laymen.

Baptists as a whole dislike any thought of church and state being officially connected. Although Baptists claim to base their whole position on the Scriptures, within the Baptist fold there are theological differences. However, it would be true to say that, speaking generally, Baptists are inclined to be more conservative theologically than some others.

In their mode of worship Baptist churches are generally speaking non-liturgical, and traditionally there has been a strong suspicion of set forms. In recent years, under the influence of the renewal movement, 'open' worship with congregational participation has been encouraged in many churches.

It is customary at the communion service in a Baptist church for two of the deacons to lead in prayers of thanksgiving for the bread and wine.

Baptists have always been concerned for religious toleration. They have not, for the most part, been so politically conscious, perhaps, as have some of the other branches of nonconformity. One of the most notable exceptions, however, was Dr John Clifford, who was noted for his vehement struggle in the early part of the century in the interests of religious education, and who championed the working classes in a number of different issues. Those who have entered the ministry in recent years tend to have a deep concern for the social implications of the gospel.

Over the years the denomination has produced some outstanding evangelical preachers, probably the most notable of them all being Charles Haddon Spurgeon, who for thirty-seven years preached weekly to a congregation of some 5,000 people. In addition he organised a college which still bears his name, and supervised the training of over 800 students. It has been said that 'Spurgeon and Clifford together sum up the Baptist denomination'.

Probably it is in the field of foreign missions that Baptists have made one of their most important contributions. It was a Baptist who earned for himself the title of 'the father of modern missions' – William Carey. There are today strong Baptist churches in many parts of the world. The Baptist Missionary Society has extensive work in India, Pakistan, Bangladesh, Malaya, Africa, the West Indies and Brazil.

A word should be said concerning those Baptist groups which are not linked with the General Baptists. The Disciples of Christ, now known in Britain as Churches of Christ, closely resemble the Baptists in doctrine and polity. They were founded by Thomas Campbell, a dynamic Irish Presbyterian. The movement began largely as a protest against the divided nature of the church and aimed to provide a simple basis of worship acceptable to all Christians. Instead, it led to the formation of yet another denomination. At various times there has been talk of a union with the Baptists, but somewhat surprisingly the Churches of Christ have now become part of the United Reformed Church. There is another small group known as Old Baptists. Old Baptists are distinctive for their practice of the laying-on of hands after baptism, although the practice of laying-on of hands after baptism is now gaining increasing acceptance in Baptist churches generally.

Mention was made earlier of the Strict and Particular Baptists, which are a distinct denomination. They now prefer to be called Grace Baptists. They practise Close Communion, such that they will only allow baptised believers to partake of the Lord's Supper, whereas in General Baptist churches the more open invitation is given to all who 'love our Lord Jesus Christ in sincerity and truth'. In the case of some Grace Baptist churches only those who are members of churches of 'the same faith and order' are admitted to the Lord's Table. The word 'particular' when used in connection with such churches refers to their doctrine of particular redemption and reveals their strong Calvinism. While General Baptists believe in general redemption the Particulars stress the doctrines of election and predestination. Many of the Strict and Particular Baptist churches are linked together in a Grace Baptist Assembly, representing some 10,000 members. The present tendency is for them to become more co-operative as far as other evangelical churches are concerned than was formerly the case.

It is estimated that there must be at least 400 Grace Baptist churches in Britain today. In 1961 the Strict Baptist Mission (now renamed Grace Baptist Mission) which ministers to Tamil-speaking people in South India and in South Malaya, celebrated its centenary. The work is supported by churches in England, and there are some thirty Grace Baptist missionaries on the field.

Undoubtedly the most important contribution Baptists have made to the church universal has been their insistence that the basis of membership must be a conscious and deliberate personal acceptance of Christ as Saviour and Lord. It is this vital evangelical experience which underlies the Baptist conception of the church and which finds expression in the ordinance of believers' baptism. At times, perhaps, they have tended to become self-conscious and have laid undue stress on the ordinance which gives them their name. It is true to say that many who do not officially belong to the Baptist fold have learned much from them, and not a few have followed their examples as to the mode of baptism while still retaining membership in other sections of the Christian church.

As with the Congregationalists, there is a group within the denomination – the Baptist Revival Fellowship – which is particularly concerned to stimulate prayer for revival and to ensure that the denomination maintains its traditional strong evangelical emphases. As a denomination, Baptists owe their origin to men who were concerned to rediscover apostolic life and faith, and it is hardly surprising that within their ranks have always been found those whose emphasis is strongly and unashamedly biblical. After all, Baptists are continually thrown back on the Bible when called upon to justify what seemed to many to be 'a strange and arbitrary idiosyncrasy'. To quote the words of a well-known Baptist theologian:

> The moral change wrought in genuine conversion, the personal repentance and faith which are the religious features of that conversion, the open confession which commits the life to a new purpose – these great truths are admirably and forcibly expressed in believers' baptism by immersion, and expressed as no other church expresses them.

The Baptist denomination has not escaped the ferment which has affected the whole church in recent years. As long ago as 1938 the Baptist Revival Fellowship was formed to stimulate prayer for revival in the denomination. In 1979 Mainstream came to birth 'to encourage new life and growth in Baptist churches in Britain'. It has grown both numerically and in influence quite remarkably in recent years. One of its leading members was elected President of the Baptist Union in 1986–87. Included in the membership of Mainstream are pastors of some of the largest Baptist churches in the country. The emphases of Mainstream are rapidly becoming accepted in the Baptist Union as a whole.

The renewal movement has made a significant impact on the denomination. Many churches have moved away from the so-called 'hymn sandwich' order of worship and are much freer in their approach. The question of eldership has been raised in some churches, and this has caused a good deal of heart-searching. Evangelism is being given a much higher profile.

As a denomination Baptists have maintained their numbers rather better than other denominations. The number of their full-time ministers is growing significantly, and their theological colleges are full to capacity.

6

Methodism

Methodism began some 200 years ago as a 'religious society' within the Church of England. Spiritual life at that time was at a low ebb. The descendants of the Puritans had largely lost their fire and were making little impact on society. In the Church of England there were some conscientious ministers of the gospel, although many were mainly interested in position and power. The historian Carlyle sums up the situation with the caustic comment, 'Soul extinct, stomach well alive.' In 1738 the Archbishop of Canterbury spoke of the age as one which displayed 'an open and professed disregard of religion'.

That same year a man was converted who, under God, was to change the face of religious life in this country, 'There was a man sent from God, whose name *was* John' (John 1:6). The two brothers, John and Charles Wesley, were sons of the Rector of Epworth in Lincolnshire. As students at Oxford University they gathered round them others who, like themselves, took their religious exercises seriously, being systematic and methodical in their way of thinking – so much so that they were dubbed 'Methodists'. It was, however, after he had left the university, been ordained as a Church of England clergyman, and gone as a missionary to Georgia, that John Wesley came into the spiritual experience that really changed his whole life. While in America he became acutely conscious of his spiritual ineffectiveness, and he returned to England.

He was greatly impressed by some Moravian missionaries he had met. It was on May 24, 1738, at a religious meeting in a house off Aldersgate Street, London, that he 'felt his heart strangely warmed'. (John Wesley's conversion is still commemorated by Methodists, who refer to May 24th as 'Wesley Day'.)

Recording the incident in his journal he adds, 'I felt I did trust in Christ, in Christ alone for my salvation, and an assurance was given me that he had taken away my sins, even mine, and saved me from the law of sin and death.' Only three days before, Charles Wesley had experienced a similar conviction through reading Luther's Commentary on the Epistle to the Galatians.

John Wesley's preaching now took on a new note and was marked by fresh power. Henceforth his labour as an evangelist knew no bounds. He became an 'apostle' to the whole nation and for fifty years travelled the country 'offering Christ'. He claimed that he taught nothing new; it was simply Scripture truth that he was propounding. He stressed instantaneous conversion and brought out of obscurity the doctrine of Christian perfection as the new convert's necessary ideal.

Wesley was more than a fiery prophet; he was also a superb organiser. He appointed lay preachers whom he sent all over the country to work in 'circuits'. He made it clear that he did not wish their preaching to be in competition with regular church services but to supplement them. He did not establish a separate church as a rival to the Church of England, to which he remained loyal all his life. He always advised his converts to receive the sacraments of the Anglican Church. However, when he died he left behind the framework of a new denomination which very soon took shape. He sponsored – especially in or near large cities such as Bristol and London – buildings for his religious societies where he and his growing band of young preachers could minister in winter, where class meetings could be held, and where young people could be taught to sing Charles Wesley's new hymns.

A word should be said here regarding Wesley's colleague,

George Whitefield. They had been fellow members of the Holy Club as students at Oxford. Whitefield was converted before the Wesleys, and he too had gone to Georgia as a missionary – although with altogether different results, preaching effectively to great crowds. When he returned to England he and John Wesley 'took sweet counsel together'.

It was said that when George Whitefield preached he could be heard a mile away. This was just as well, for many pulpits were closed to him and, like the Wesleys, he found himself very often preaching in the open air. Thousands of people would stand spellbound by his message, and many turned to Christ, repenting of their sins. In six weeks the whole district in and around Bristol was stirred through his ministry until 'men talked of nothing but religion'.

In 1741, however, Wesley clashed with Whitefield over the doctrine of predestination. While in America Whitefield had been much influenced by the Calvinism of Jonathan Edwards. Wesley could not accept this doctrine. Both men held that salvation was free to any and all who believe. Where Whitefield and Wesley differed was in their view of the ultimate source of saving faith. Wesley held that in the last resort salvation was determined by the will of the sinner, whereas Whitefield taught that it was determined by the will of God. Whitefield found much help from the wealthy Countess of Huntingdon, who gave her jewels and much of her wealth to further his work. Through her instrumentality many chapels were built. Let it be said that Wesley and Whitefield remained firm friends and 'agreed to disagree' over the question of election and predestination. When Whitefield died nearly thirty years later it was John Wesley who gave the address at his funeral.

It was in London that the first Society of Inquirers came together to meet John Wesley week by week, 'a company of men having the form and seeking the power of godliness'. As the number grew he divided them into classes of about twelve persons in each and appointed a leader to every class. It was the business of the leader to see every person in his class once a week at least in order to inquire how their souls prospered, and to advise and comfort as the occasion might require. Week by week, the leader was also to receive from each member what they were willing to give towards the relief of the poor and to hand this money over to the stewards of the Society. Membership of the Society could only be retained by an upright manner of life, by regularity in attendance at Holy Communion and by private prayer and Bible study. It was impossible for John and Charles Wesley and their occasional helpers among the clergy adequately to minister to the spiritual needs of the societies, and when gifted preachers arose among the societies themselves John Wesley felt that they should be encouraged to exercise their gifts. As the societies grew, it was necessary that more and more of these laymen should give their whole time up to the work, and so the Methodist Conference came into being. In June 1744 John Wesley called his first conference of preachers at the London headquarters – the Foundry, Moorfields. The conference that year consisted of a small group of ordained clergymen of the Church of England and a few itinerant lay preachers.

The need of these growing and widespread societies led Wesley to build up an organisation somewhat similar to the Presbyterian system. He believed from his study of the Scriptures that bishops and presbyters were essentially of the same order and therefore had the same right to ordain. For many years he denied himself that right in his desire 'not to violate the established order of the national church'. Later, however, he found himself compelled by circumstances to ordain his own preachers for the work of the ministry, first for America, then for Scotland, and finally for England. He was not content to stand aside indefinitely and see his people deprived of the sacraments because of the unwillingness of bishops to ordain his preachers. This step taken by Wesley, of course, was destined to lead to a break with the Church of England, although he himself declared at the end of his life, 'I never had any design of separating from the church....I declare once more that I live and die a member of the Church of England.' Methodists have always felt a close affinity with the Church of

England, and are reluctant to some extent to be bracketed with other nonconformist bodies.

After Wesley's death there were considerable differences of opinion among his followers. In 1797 a Methodist New Connexion was founded, largely due to the zeal of Alexander Kilham, one of Wesley's travelling preachers, who desired all connection with the Church of England to end. The Primitive Methodists owe their origin largely to a great open-air camp meeting called Mow Cop, which was held on the top of a hill near the Potteries in 1807. Their leaders, Hugh Bourne and William Clowes, gathered together a church composed largely of working men who had been untouched by the mainstream of Wesleyanism. In their keenness for evangelism the Primitive Methodists were prepared to adopt certain methods which did not commend themselves to Methodists as a whole, encouraging 'camp meetings' which attracted great crowds to listen to 'revival addresses'. The first leaders of the British Labour movement were largely drawn from the ranks of the Primitive Methodists. In the West country the Bible Christians were the outcome of a spiritual awakening at Shebbear in North Devon. In 1932 all the main Methodist denominations – the Wesleyan Methodists, the Primitive Methodists and United Methodists – came together to form the Methodist Church in Great Britain. To this day, however, there are still traces of the early divisions, and in some localities there are reduntant churches as a result.

A word should be added here regarding the Independent Methodists, a body that still maintains its own identity. This name was officially adopted in 1898 to describe those who at different times and in different areas had also been known as Quaker-Methodists or Singing Methodists. Some churches were also called Christian Lay Churches. The distinctive features of the Independent Methodists are their strong belief in independency as regards church government, and in a voluntary and unpaid ministry. Independent Methodism is strongest in the north of England. They have in all about 115 churches comprising a membership of over 4,000.

A somewhat similar body and comparable in size and influence (but recognising an ordained ministry) is the Wesleyan Reform Union. The largest church is in Sheffield, where the denomination's headquarters are situated. The Wesleyan Reform Union expresses its missionary interest through a number of different interdenominational societies.

The Free Methodist Church was established in the United Kingdom in 1960. It has about 20 churches and some 800 members. Its main base is in the United States.

The world Methodist community consists of some 40,000,000 people of whom over 19,000,000 are church members, about 450,000 being in the British Isles. These members are distributed among some 8,000 churches, each with a church council to care for its spiritual life and to look after the fabric. The church council is composed of the church stewards (or chief officers), the class leader (whose job it is to keep in touch with the dozen or so church members on their class books) and the leaders of the chief departments of the church and others chosen by the annual society meeting of all the members.

The 8,000 churches of Methodism are grouped together in circuits, each of which has a quarterly meeting over which the superintendent minister presides. He may have a considerable number of churches under his care. He will also have several ministerial colleagues, each of whom will be specially attached to one or several of the churches in the circuit, but all of them, including the superintendent, will be available to take services in the different churches. On the Sundays when the services are not taken by an ordained minister, one of Methodism's army of local preachers will occupy the pulpit. Circuits are linked together in districts, with synods made up of all the ministers and many laymen meeting twice a year under the chairmanship of the chairman of the district, who does not have other pastoral duties but is the full-time officer of the Synod – a sort of Methodist 'bishop'.

The Methodist Conference, which is the highest authority in Methodism, meets for one week each summer. It is made up of 288 ministers and 288 laymen and is presided over by the president of the conference who must be a minister. The vice-president is chosen from among the lay members of the church. Ministers are ordained at the conference, and the first woman minister was ordained in 1974.

Methodist ministers are usually regarded as being far more mobile than their colleagues in the other free churches. Normally the appointment of a minister to a circuit is for an initial period of five years. Thereafter the invitation may be renewed annually. The Methodist minister is provided with a furnished house by the circuit.

The Overseas Division of the Methodist Church operates in Africa, India, Sri Lanka, West Africa, Hong Kong, South-East Asia and the Caribbean, with over 550 missionaries helping to care for some 700,000 Methodists overseas.

What of Methodism today? In Britain, as I have already pointed out, Methodism remains the strongest numerically of the free churches. In theory at least Methodism stands where it has always stood theologically. In practice it would be true to say, as in other free churches, that there are considerable divergences on theological matters, ranging from fundamentalism to extreme liberalism. However, there is within the denomination a solid body of men and women who still believe that the secret of Methodism lies in its emphasis on the need for personal faith in a personal Saviour.

Methodism has never been fond of theological controversy. John Wesley himself found no fault with the Thirty-nine Articles of the Church of England and always contended that he was only preaching what he had learned as a minister in that church. In the early days Methodists were far more concerned with the experience of personal salvation and evangelism than with entering into theological discussion. In more recent years there has been a tendency in the denomination to dwell upon the social implications of the gospel. Many have turned to schemes of world betterment and social uplift and some would think that in so doing they have tended to overlook the New Testament emphasis on personal salvation. However, there is undoubtedly much that evangelicals generally can learn from Methodism's concern to apply the gospel to life. John Wesley taught his people from the start to be concerned for education. In the nineteenth century Methodists were to the fore as exponents of the 'nonconformist conscience'. Over recent years Methodist conferences have included in their debates such topics as industry and the social order, nuclear disarmament, drug abuse, gambling, the use of Sunday, marriage and divorce, and AIDS.

Methodists have succeeded where other free churches have failed in some of the 'down-town' areas of our great cities. Their Central Halls have ministered both to the spiritual and physical needs of the community, and although today many of them are in decline, nevertheless they have in many cases a history of which they can be justly proud. Methodist homes for the aged are also a credit to the denomination. Probably more Methodists than other free churchmen give their time and talents to the service to the community in public work, whether in local government, in trade unions or in the House of Commons. The Division of Social Responsibility of the Methodist Church was set up to convey to the government the view of Methodists on various social questions.

Methodism is clearly the most highly organised of all the denominations. Its Home Mission Division promotes evangelistic work in Great Britain and tackles tasks considered to be beyond the capacity of the local circuit. The Division of Ministries is concerned for the training and employment of ministers as well as local preachers upon whom Methodism depends so greatly for the conduct of Sunday services. The Ministerial Training Department looks after the theological colleges at: Bristol; Leeds; The Queen's College, Birmingham, a joint Anglican-Methodist venture; and Wesley House, Cambridge. The National Children's Home is also a Methodist foundation. There are Methodist day schools and boarding schools, and two colleges of education: Westminster College at Oxford, and Southlands College at Wimbledon. There is also an Order of Deacons for the training of men and women to be mainly full-time servants of the church. The weekly Methodist Recorder has a larger circulation than any other Protestant paper in Britain.

Methodism has its quota of pressure groups. The Methodist Sacramental Fellowship is particularly interested in promoting sacramental teaching within the denomination, whilst the Radical Group, as its name implies, represents more the 'left wing' in the denomination. The Methodist Revival Fellowship was formed in 1955 to encourage prayer for revival and to emphasise the need for scriptural holiness. In 1970 Conservative Evangelicals in Methodism was launched to 'conserve biblical truth' within the denomination. Happily in 1987 these two bodies merged under the new name of 'Headway'.

Cliff College in Derbyshire is a name familiar to many outside the boundaries of Methodism. Thousands of people have come under its influence through its seaside campaigns and evangelistic missions. Although set up for the training of lay evangelists many of its students have later entered the Methodist ministry or gone overseas as missionaries. Its annual 'open day' attracts thousands of visitors when well-known preachers may be heard expounding the gospel in the college's glorious setting amongst the Derbyshire hills.

Methodism in certain respects has somewhat closer affinities with Anglicanism than the other free churches. While an ordained minister is not referred to as a 'priest', he normally conducts a Communion Service, although in special circumstances a lay preacher may be given permission to do so. Within the denomination there are two main schools of thought – those who prefer 'free' worship similar to that enjoyed in other nonconformist churches, and those who opt for a more set form of liturgy. The Methodist Service Book, issued in 1974 and authorised by Conference, contains orders of service used in many Methodist churches. The annual Covenant Service, held at the beginning of each year, is peculiar to Methodism, and on this occasion every church member renews his or her vows of allegiance to the Lord and to his church.

The Methodist Hymn Book, published in 1933, has been widely acclaimed as one of the best hymn books available, used in churches outside the denomination as well. However, this has now been superseded by 'Hymns and Psalms', published in 1983, which was intended to be more 'ecumenical' in outlook and includes some more modern hymns.

Methodists as a whole have consistently favoured the aims and objectives of the ecumenical movement. As long ago as 1955 machinery was set in motion which it was hoped would eventually lead to full communion with the Church of England and ultimately organic union. Although both Anglican Convocations and successive Methodist Conferences welcomed the scheme which was presented to them, it was rejected because it failed to gain the required majority from the Anglican side. This was a bitter blow to Methodism.

The renewal movement has in recent years had a significant influence in Methodist churches. Some churches which appeared 'dead' have 'come alive'. In some cases division has resulted – the new wine has not been contained happily in the old wineskins – but certainly within the denomination there is a renewed emphasis on spiritual life and evangelistic outreach. The old 'class meeting' is being reborn with the formation of house groups, and many of the men and women coming out of the theological colleges have a deep concern for the spiritual life of the denomination.

7

The Society of Friends (Quakers)

The Society of Friends – more popularly known as the Quakers – might be said to represent the extreme left-wing of the
English Reformation. Indeed, their originator George Fox
(1621–1691) has been called 'a nonconformist to nonconformity'. Fox reacted against all theological and institutional
expressions of Christianity and maintained that 'every man
was enlighted by the Divine Light of Christ'. Ecclesiastical
systems and organisations were anathema to him, whether
Catholic or Protestant.

Fox and his followers ceased from 'the teachings of all men
and their words, and their worships, and their temples, and all
their baptisms and churches', and 'met together often and
waited upon the Lord in pure silence from our own words and
all men's words, and hearkened to the voice of the Lord, and
felt his word in our hearts to burn up and beat down all that
was contrary to God.'

Fox himself was an unconventional figure. He was
extremely forthright in his criticism of institutional Christianity and referred, somewhat contemptuously, to the churches
in his day as 'steeple-houses'. He and his followers adopted
their own peculiar manner of speech, form of dress and
behaviour in society. He taught his followers to address one
another in the second person singular (thou, thee, etc) and to
dress with the utmost simplicity. Fox declared that it was quite

impossible for a Christian to participate in war under any circumstances or to swear an oath. From the beginning, the Quakers showed a deep concern for social righteousness, Fox himself being particularly troubled about prison conditions in his day. He encouraged his followers to engage with the utmost industry in their particular trade or profession, for by this means they would be in a position to give generously to those who were in need.

When the issue of slavery came to the fore in the late eighteenth century, the Quakers played a prominent part. Also at this time the Quakers were enthusiastic supporters of the adult schools which were being started in many places, primarily to help those who had not the benefits of any education as youngsters to learn to read and write. It is often stated that the name 'Quaker' came to be given to Fox and his followers because of the great emotion which they frequently displayed, especially at their informal meetings for prayer. It seems, however, that the nickname was first given by Justice Bennet in 1650 to George Fox because he bade the Justice 'tremble' at the Word of the Lord. The Quakers became the subject of the most bitter persecution – George Fox himself spending a total of eight years in different prisons. They were persecuted by Dissenters and Anglicans alike because of the attitude they adopted toward credal Christianity. However, their numbers increased until they reached their peak of 60,000 members at the end of the seventeenth century.

Since then, however, the movement has declined considerably, although it would be true to say that its influence has been far beyond its numerical strength. Between 1650 and 1698 no fewer than 15,000 Quakers suffered death for their faith; others were whipped, tortured, or had their ears cut off. In both England and America, people who helped or harboured them were severely punished for 'collaborating in heresy and treason'. In spite of the bitter opposition they met at every turn, Fox and his followers remained true to what they believed. They would not pay taxes used to support 'the state-paid clergy'. They wore broad-brimmed hats which they refused to doff before anyone, whether magistrate, clergyman or king.

The Quakers maintain that the 'inward light' is their direct source of the divine knowledge and is higher than the testimony of Scripture and superior to reason or conscience, and all credal formulations of Christianity. It is not surprising perhaps that over the centuries Quakers have as a whole drifted somewhat from the basic doctrines of the Christian faith. Some have inclined towards Unitarianism.

From time to time there have been protests from within their own ranks at this tendency and movements have sprung up to redress the balance. We might mention here a group that has certain affinities with the Society of Friends, although not officially linked with them, bearing the name Friends' Evangelistic Band. This has now been renamed the Fellowship for Evangelising Britain's Villages. The Band had its birth in a fellowship of prayer for spiritual awakening in the Society of Friends. It later outgrew denominational boundaries and welcomed men and women from all the evangelical churches in its ranks. Considerable support for the work does in fact come from Friends in Northern Ireland. The main objective of the Band was to evangelise and to maintain a living gospel witness in the villages of England. In pursuit of this objective, Band missionaries have been sent forth to work in different villages. Every member of the Band lives 'by faith' and looks to God alone to supply his needs. This continues to be the policy of the FEBV.

It would not be right to give the impression that there are no evangelical Christians in the ranks of the Society of Friends. It is interesting to recall that one of the founders of the Keswick Convention was a Quaker. In the USA there are groups of Friends who maintain a strong evangelical witness, some of whom – for example, the Ohio Yearly Meeting – are actively linked with the National Association of Evangelicals, the American counterpart of the Evangelical Alliance. In this context we might refer to a group about which little is known in England – the Mennonites.

The Mennonites, it has been said, come somewhere between the Baptists and Quakers, seeking to be as evangelical as the Baptists and as radical in applying the gospel to social questions as the Quakers. Originating in Switzerland in 1515, they follow the teaching of Menno Simons. In Europe they are mainly to be found in the Netherlands and North-East Germany. They are evangelical in their theology but follow a number of practices which are not widely found in today's church, such as foot-washing. They require women to cover their heads at worship services and insist on soberness of attire. Mennonites do not engage in military service, nor do they take oaths in a court of law. Most practise baptism by pouring rather than immersion, and they observe the Lord's Supper twice a year. Each church is independent and free to choose its own minister. There are about 400,000 Mennonites in the world today, 250,000 of whom are in the United States of America. They are, in fact, descendants of the sixteenth century Anabaptists and were from the outset a radical free church. They see the church as a closely knit missionary brotherhood, where there is no distinction between clergy and laity. In 1940 a small group of Mennonites established themselves in England, and in London there is today a small Mennonite fellowship responsible for running an international students' hostel.

In England today there are probably about 16,000 Quakers, with an equally large number of 'attenders' – those who, while not in actual membership, fully associate with Friends in their work and worship, often at the same time retaining their membership in other churches. The Independent Methodist Churches, which are mostly to be found in the north of England, grew out of Quakerism and retain close links with the Society of Friends. The largest yearly meeting of Friends in the world is in Kenya – the result of mission work begun by American Friends in 1902. Altogether there are over 30,000 Friends in East Africa.

Popular ideas about Quakers are extremely diverse. Some conjure up a picture of a remote figure of the past, entirely otherworldly and dressed in somewhat strange, though plain garb. Others recognise contemporary Friends as being a small, numerically negligible coterie who cherish high ethical standards and indulge in the habit of waiting together in private for divine inspiration and comfort.

Often a Quaker meeting-house is very difficult to find, and when it is eventually reached it is usually far from prepossessing in appearance. The appointed room in which meetings for worship take place is bare except for rows of benches parallel to each of the four walls (or chairs may be used), leaving a small square in the centre where there is a table on which reposes a Bible. The company gather at the appointed hour in silence and the meeting usually lasts about an hour. Much of that time is spent in silence, although anyone present is free to express himself vocally in prayer or in words of exhortation or reflection. There is no minister in charge, no communion table, no choir, no organ or piano, and no pulpit. The sacraments of baptism and the Lord's Supper are spiritualised and find no tangible expression as far as Quaker practice is concerned. The outward manifestations which are said to have led originally to the use of the name 'Quaker' – ie, trembler – are rarely known among Friends today.

George Fox, who was a born organiser, saw the need to have some loose organisation to wield a somewhat individualistic people into a fellowship. He worked out a system of local, district and national meetings to which the Society of Friends still adheres. Men and women are on equal terms in church affairs, and there is no responsibility or office that cannot be held by either. Decisions at meetings are taken only on the basis of unanimity.

Quakers, because of their dislike of church organisation and failure to make outward use of sacraments, as well as their strong pacifist leanings, have frequently been misunderstood by members of other Christian denominations. Undoubtedly, Quakerism at its best demands a remarkably high degree of spirituality. It is hardly surprising that the movement has suffered periodically from losing that spiritual exultation which is its essential prerequisite. At times it seems that Quakers have largely confined their Christian enthusiasm to social questions, relief and other humanitarian work. In this field they have an unparalleled record. The Friends' Service Council has done all in its power to foster interracial, international and inter-tribal understanding in various parts of the world. Thousands of pounds have been spent on community work of various kinds, including refugee work, the running of international centres, rural schools and other educational establishments. In the two great wars many conscientious objectors found themselves serving with some of the Friends' ambulance units which did such fine work in the different theatres of war. Woodbrooke College in Birmingham is a Quaker foundation, as are several well-known schools.

The Society of Friends was largely unaffected by the evangelical revival which made such an impact on other branches of nonconformity. It should be said, however, that Quakers as a whole gave a lead in the matter of the abolition of slavery. As long ago as 1641 George Fox had urged Friends in the West Indies to treat their slaves with humanity, and the Quakers were among the first to become sensitive to the whole question of the slave traffic. In 1758 and again in 1761 London Quakers drew public attention to the iniquities of the system. In 1774 any Friend who persisted in having dealings with the slave trade was expelled from the Society. Undoubtedly their strong action on behalf of the slaves brought the Quakers into a position of leadership in social questions which they have retained to some extent ever since.

Over the years the Society of Friends has produced some outstanding politicians, the most noble of whom was William Penn, who did so much to establish the ideals of the Society of Friends on both sides of the Atlantic. Another Friend who became prominent in politics was John Bright. In the last century, too, there have risen from their ranks some notable figures in British industry. These men have set a noble example in the way they conducted their affairs and have been greatly respected for their integrity. Familiar names in the confectionery world – Fry's, Rowntree's and Cadbury's – have all had close associations with the Society of Friends. Other notable Quakers include: Elizabeth Fry (1780–1845), the prison reformer; Joseph Lancaster (1778–1838), the pioneer of elementary education; and the Lloyd family, founders of the bank which still bears that name. A number of outstanding scientists, Fellows of the Royal Society, have been members of the Society of Friends.

Quakers see themselves as representing a third stream of Christianity, distinct from both the Catholic and Reformed traditions. Their aim has always been to re-discover primitive Christianity unencumbered by subsequent church tradition.

In summary, we may say that we owe to the Quakers their strong emphasis upon the doctrine of the Holy Spirit – the 'inward light' – and also their concern for the social implications of the gospel. It is to be regretted that today the Society of Friends seems for the most part to have moved away from its essential spiritual emphasis and to have allowed, to some extent, its social concern to outweigh its pietism.

Perhaps we may best assess the present situation, so far as the Religious Society of Friends is concerned, by referring to a press advertisement, in which it was stated:

Quakers are not, as cereal packets suggest to some, quaintly dressed puritans, or fanatical sabbatarians who say 'no' to everything from whist to war. Quakerism has always been a modern faith, concerned with living a seven-day week Christianity in the world today rather than trying to compress belief into a formula.

It is indicative of the social and political interests of Friends that there exist such groups as Quaker Peace and Service, involved in peace work in Britain and overseas, Quaker Social Responsibility and Education, Quaker work camps, short-term community service projects with international groups of volunteers, and Quaker Concern for Animal Welfare which actively opposes vivisection. The Friends Vegetarian Society promotes vegetarianism as being a better way of life. There is also a Friends Homosexual Fellowship.

There is an inevitable gulf between those who emphasise the importance of sound doctrine and the Quaker outlook which repudiates creeds and doctrinal bases. Nevertheless, we should be ready to concede that the practical application of the gospel, which is the hallmark of Quakerism, is something that has not always been as carefully observed by some Christians as it might have been. It would also be true to say that the Society of Friends has played a part in English religious life totally disproportionate to the number within the fellowship.

8

Small Denominations and Ethnic Churches

We shall be considering now a number of different denominations which, although relatively small numerically, are extremely interesting historically and from the standpoint of their spiritual contribution.

The Moravian Church

The Moravian Church, the oldest free church in Northern Europe, was founded in 1457 in Bohemia and Moravia, sixty years before the great Protestant Reformation began. It arose out of the work and teaching of John Hus who was martyred in 1415, and who was himself inspired and influenced by John Wyclif, the English reformer who lived and taught in the fourteenth century, often referred to as 'The Morning Star of the Reformation'.

The Moravian Church used to be known as the Unitas Fratrum, or 'Fellowship of Brethren'. It has been established in England for more than two centuries, being recognised by an Act of Parliament in 1749 as a Protestant Episcopal church. It shared in the great evangelical revival of the eighteenth century and was the first Protestant church to begin foreign mission work, in 1732.

The church is governed by general and provincial synods composed of ministerial and lay representatives. The orders of the ministry are those of deacon, presbyter and bishop. Ordination is by the bishop. The bishops are chosen and elected by the provincial synods but are regarded as bishops of the whole church. The Holy Scriptures are the only rule of faith and practice. The form of service used is not unlike that of the Book of Common Prayer, but while liturgical forms are used, provision is also made for the use of extempore prayer. The service of Holy Communion is open to those of other denominations.

The British province of the Moravian Church consists of nearly forty congregations with over thirty ministers. The communicant membership is just under 3,000. The legislative body of the province is the provincial synod which now meets once every two years.

The British province of the Moravian church is responsible for missionary work in Tanzania, Labrador, Jamaica and India. The financial support of this work has been greatly assisted by an interdenominational society founded by a Church of England clergyman in 1817, known as the London Association in Aid of Moravian Missions.

Moravians as such have no particular doctrinal teachings which stamp them as a denomination. Their whole emphasis has been upon practical Christianity rather than doctrinal forms. It is said that when the original Moravians withdrew from the Church of Rome it was not primarily for theological reasons, but on moral grounds. They formed an independent church, not to promulgate new doctrines but to show forth in living together fundamental Christian fellowship. Traditionally, Moravians have laid stress on 'conduct rather than creed'. It is claimed that their church, while it has always been grounded in the Christian faith, has stressed those points of doctrine which unite the followers of our Lord rather than those which cause dissension. While they consistently claim that 'the Holy Scriptures are our only rule of faith and practice' they do not subscribe to any particular theory of inspiration, nor do they give any precise indication as to how the Scriptures are to be interpreted.

To sum up their position in the words of the church itself:

The Moravian Church is an ancient episcopal and evangelical church; her head is Christ; her stand is the Bible; her members are a fellowship of believers; her life is the service of God and our fellow men across the world; and her continuing and distinctive purpose has been to witness to the unity of all Christians and all the churches in the fellowship of Christ.

The Lutheran Church

One of the smallest yet most historic Protestant churches in Britain is the Evangelical Lutheran Church of England. In the sixteenth century it appeared that the Lutheran faith might become the common religion of the British people. 1673 saw the consecration of the first Lutheran church in Britain in the city of London. Over the years a number of other congregations were formed, largely to cater for Lutherans from the continent of Europe domiciled in England.

The Evangelical Lutheran Church of England – a purely British endeavour – came to birth in 1896 and is a free and independent self-supporting church, affiliated to the Missouri Synod of Lutherans of the USA. There is also a United Lutheran Synod, distinct from the Evangelical Lutheran Church of England but linked with the Lutheran World Federation. This body is mainly concerned with work amongst refugees from the continent, of whom there are some 20,000 – though the Polish group has now transferred to the Evangelical Lutheran Church of England.

So far in Britain, the Lutheran Church of England numbers less than twenty congregations with over 1,000 communicant members, although there are in addition a number of 'mission stations'. There are some fifteen to twenty pastors. There is one Lutheran Church in Dublin and a number of churches catering for Lutherans in exile from the Baltic countries.

Lutherans are strong in their biblical emphasis and sub-

scribe to the Augsburg Confession of 1529 as well as accepting
the general credal statements of the primitive church. They
reject the doctrine of 'apostolic succession' as popularly
understood, claiming that the New Testament terms 'bishop',
'elder' and 'pastor' are descriptive of one and the same office.

In the Lutheran form of church government the local congregation conducts its own affairs and chooses its own pastor.
Congregations may choose to delegate some of their authority
to others, but those who act on their behalf do so solely by
transferred right. They practise infant baptism and adhere to
traditional Lutheran teaching as to the real presence of Christ
in the Lord's Supper. Lutherans are amillennialists as far as
their understanding of prophecy is concerned, rejecting the
theory of a literal reign of Christ for 1,000 years upon the
earth. Generally speaking they take a strong line in regard to
Freemasonry, claiming that the religion of the Masonic Order
is deistic but antichristian in character.

The Lutherans in Britain are strong believers in the use of
modern means of communication for the propagation of the
gospel. They distribute films and filmstrips ('Concordia') in
great quantities and have an active interest in the Lutheran
Hour radio programme, 'Bringing Christ to the Nations'.

The Countess of Huntingdon's Connexion

As the Confessional Articles of her Connexion make plain,
the Countess of Huntingdon stood in the Calvinist tradition.
She had early association with the Wesleys, but as time went
on she favoured more and more the emphasis made by
George Whitefield, who became her chaplain in 1748.

Undoubtedly the Countess was the most remarkable
woman of her generation. Born into the aristocracy, she pos-
sessed an acute mind, remarkable administrative ability and a
unique gift for reaching those of her own station in life with
the gospel. She sent her preachers throughout the length and
breadth of the country to proclaim the gospel and call sinners
to repentance. While she herself was a loyal member of the

Church of England, her zeal was such that she soon found herself frustrated by the prevailing ecclesiastical system, with the
result that, to her great regret, she eventually found herself
compelled to secede from the church. The immediate circumstances leading to her secession concerned Northampton
Chapel, Spa Fields, which she had opened as a 'Temple of
God' in 1777. The phenomenal success of the work there was
not appreciated by the local clergyman, who obtained an
ecclesiastical court order requiring the chapel to be closed.
Undaunted, the Countess reopened the chapel in 1779 as a
free church, although the service continued to be conducted
in accordance with the Book of Common Prayer. The local
vicar objected to the fact that Church of England clergymen
were engaged to preach there, and eventually the Countess
felt she had no other course left but to leave the church she
loved.

In the following years, chapels were erected in many different towns and cities of England, in which the liturgical service of the Church of England was followed and the gospel
preached in all its fullness. Church forms and usages were
observed and the Countess did all she could not to widen the
gulf. In order, however, to train ministers for her pulpits she
established a college at Trevecca, South Wales, with Fletcher
of Madeley as its first president. The college later transferred
to Cheshunt, Hertfordshire, and in the early part of the present century was established in Cambridge with the name
Cheshunt College.

The history of the missionary outreach of the churches
associated with the Countess is fascinating. During the American War of Independence many negroes fought on the side of
the British and as a reward for their services were promised liberty. After the declaration of peace in 1783 they were sent to
Nova Scotia. Here they were ministered to by men who had
been trained at the Countess's college in Wales, and a Christian community made up of freed slaves grew up in Nova
Scotia. In 1792, of the 2,000 of these freed slaves settled on the
west coast of Africa by the British Government, over a

thousand claimed to be members of the Countess of Huntingdon's Connexion. It was not, however, till 1899 that the first white missionary superintendent was sent from England to Sierra Leone. Over the years the churches of the Connexion have maintained a lively interest in their sister churches in Sierra Leone.

It is estimated that the countess's efforts in Britain led to the opening of no less than 200 chapels and missions throughout the country, and in 1828, nearly forty years after her death, there were estimated to be some 35,000 regularly attending these chapels, with seventy-two officiating ministers. Over the years many of these chapels have closed and others have been absorbed into the larger denominations. Today there are less than thirty churches and missions in the Connexion, with twenty-two ministers or evangelists in charge and a total membership of about 800. None of the churches now adhere to a liturgical form of service.

The Countess of Huntingdon's Connexion, although small today, has a proud history and is one of the fruits of the evangelical revival. If God should be pleased to send his people another such revival one may well expect to see this group of churches entering fully into it.

The Free Church of England

This church was founded in 1844, largely in reaction to the growing influence of the Tractarian or Oxford Movement in the Church of England. There were evangelical clergy in the church who felt that the underlying purpose of the Oxford Movement was to bring the church back to the position that it held prior to the Reformation, and to restore the ritual and practices of Rome. The Free Church of England actually began in the West Country, following the secession from the Church of England of the Rev James Shore, minister of Bridgetown Chapel-of-ease, Totnes. Shortly afterwards, churches were established in Exeter and in Ilfracombe. A number of other churches sprang up independently in various parts of the country. In the early days there was close collaboration with the Countess of Huntingdon's Connexion, with which the Free Church of England has close affinities.

As time went on the leaders of the Countess of Huntingdon's Connexion inclined more towards Congregationalism and it soon became clear that the Connexion and the Free Church of England must go their separate ways.

In 1863 a constitution for the newly formed Free Church of England was duly registered in the High Court of Chancery. This new branch of the Church of God was now established with a Presbyterian ministry, a recognition of and provision for episcopacy, and pledged to the doctrines of the Church of England as set forth in the Thirty-nine Articles of Religion. The Free Church of England has always attempted to combine what it considered was best in the episcopal, Presbyterian and Congregational systems of church government. It is episcopal in the sense that one of the presbyters, chosen by his fellow presbyters and the deacons assembled in convocation, is deemed to have the oversight of all the congregations in a district or diocese, and one of them in particular is chosen by convocation as the president or bishop primus of the whole denomination.

In 1874 news reached this country of the formation of the Reformed Episcopal Church in America under the leadership of Bishop Cummins. Incidentally, one of the factors leading up to the bishop's secession from the American Episcopal Church was his participation in a United Communion Service in New York in 1873 held under the auspices of the Evangelical Alliance.

It was clear that the Reformed Episcopal Church was substantially the same in outlook as the Free Church of England, and a working arrangement was soon made between the two churches, leading eventually to union in 1927. This body claims to have preserved the 'historic episcopate'.

From the beginning both the Free Church of England and the Reformed Episcopal Church have shown a strong missionary interest. In the early days the Free Church of England joined with the Countess of Huntingdon's Connexion in supporting the Sierra Leone Mission, but in 1920 the principal interest of the Free Church of England was transferred to the China Inland Mission. In more recent years several other evangelical missionary societies have shared the interest of the church. In 1958, convocation decreed that the three societies officially supported by the Free Church of England were to be the China Inland Mission, the South African General Mission and the Moravian Missionary Society. It should be added that it has been a tradition in the Free Church of England for many years to invite a bishop of the Moravian Church to assist in the consecration of its own bishops.

The Free Church of England recognises two dioceses, the northern and the southern. It might be noted, in passing, that the late Dr William Culbertson, President of the Moody Bible Institute in Chicago, was formerly Presiding Bishop of the Reformed Episcopal Church in America. Candidates for the ministry in this country are encouraged to seek training under the auspices of the London Bible College.

The position of the Free Church of England is unique. It stands midway between the established church and those free churches having a liturgical form of worship. It has endeavoured not to enter into competition with any evangelical church in any town or city. Generally speaking, churches have been founded in response to appeals from groups of church people who have found themselves driven out of their spiritual home by ritualistic innovations in their parish churches.

It should be said that the Free Church of England, although clearly founded on evangelical lines, has not had the support that one might have imagined. Indeed, in many quarters it has aroused considerable hostility, sometimes due to ignorance of its history or to misunderstanding of its mission, and sometimes because of its tendency to an extreme Protestantism – for instance, the wearing of surplices by the choir is forbidden by canon. Many who have served in its ministry have later been ordained in the Church of England. There are at present

about thirty churches of the Free Church of England throughout the country.

Some ethnic churches

There are in Britain a number of relatively small churches catering for different ethnic groups. Of these the Chinese Church
is one of the largest and most active. Services are held in several locations in London as well as in other large cities. In all
the membership of the church is in the region of 5,000 with a
number of full-time workers. The Chinese Overseas Christian
Mission, under the direction of Mary Wang, seeks to establish
Chinese churches in the United Kingdom as well as on the
continent of Europe. These are all firmly rooted in the
evangelical tradition.

There are at least one million Asians living in Britain. This
number consists of many different nationalities and religions
– Hindus, Muslims, Sikhs, secularists and materialists. Even
the Christians among them are divided by origin, language
and denomination. For example, there are Syrian congregations in Britain which remain distinctly Syrian. They worship
in Malayalam and intermarry within their own community.

Various Christian fellowships exist to provide a rallying point
for Christians, particularly students from overseas. Thus there is
the Ghana Christian Fellowship, Hong Kong Christian Fellowship, Indian Christian Organisaton, Malaysian Christian
Fellowship, Overseas Fellowship of Nigerian Christians,
Indonesian Christian Fellowship, Iranian Christian Fellowship,
and the Christian Arab Fellowship – all endeavouring to express
love and give encouragement to Christian nationals studying or
working in the United Kingdom. There is also in London both
a Japanese and a Korean Christian church.

There are Protestant churches for French and Spanish
speaking members of the community. There are also Roman
Catholic churches catering for different nationalities – Croa-
tian, German, Hungarian, Italian, Latvian, Lithuanian,
Slovene and Ukrainian.

The Eastern Orthodox churches are also represented in Britain. The Greek Orthodox Church has more than 100,000 members active here. Other Orthodox churches include the Russian, Bulgarian, Coptic, Esthonian, Ethiopian, Latvian, Polish, Rumanian, Serbian, Syrian and Ukrainian. Orthodox worship tends to be highly ritualistic. Their churches are full of icons – colourful pictures and images – which are venerated by the congregation.

Over the years many small independent episcopal churches have come on the scene. Some have proved to be 'paper churches' and disappeared almost as quickly as they grew up. They claim to share with the Roman Catholic Church, the Church of England and the Eastern Orthodox Church the traditional historic apostolic succession. Sadly at times public attention has been drawn to such churches when the misdemeanours of one of their 'bishops' have come to public notice. In most cases such groups have only one or two different places of worship and their influence is very limited. They exist on very slender financial resources and usually their clergy are non-stipendiary. There are those, for example, who refer to themselves as 'old Roman Catholics' with their own archbishop, and 'liberal' Catholics with up to twenty congregations.

One of the most fascinating stories is that of the Catholic Apostolic Church, founded in the 1830s. One of its earliest leaders was Edward Irving, a friend of Henry Drummond and himself an evangelical. Irving was repudiated by the London presbytery when he became involved with speaking in tongues and divine healing. He preached that the 'day of the Lord' was near and under 'prophetic direction' he and his followers set apart twelve latter-day apostles. The community proceeded to adopt elaborate ritual similar to that being fostered by the Tractarian movement. It spread to the continent of Europe and beyond, but today the church numbers less than 2,000.

9

Black-Led Churches

We might well wonder why so many calypso-singing West Indians should leave their sun-drenched islands in the Caribbean and settle here in cold and often unwelcoming Britain. Why have Asians left India and Pakistan, and also East Africa, to live in Britain, often settling in run-down areas of our big industrial cities? The answer in both cases lies in the field of politics and economics.

The hurricane damage in Jamaica in 1951 was a factor behind a large influx of West Indians to Britain in the subsequent years. After partition in India and the riots accompanying it, many came to Britain in search of a more stable way of life. The atrocities in Uganda associated with Idi Amin drove many Asians living in that country to seek refuge over here. In 1950 there were only approximately 100,000 coloured people living in Britain. The influx of immigrants from Commonwealth countries grew rapidly from 1954 onwards. Betwen 1957 and 1966 the coloured population of Britain doubled, now that West Indians were joined by immigrants from India and Pakistan. This is not the place to discuss the various laws which have been enacted since then to limit numbers.

Many of those who came to these shores, especially those from the West Indies, had a strong Christian background back home. They naturally explored the possibilities of becoming integrated into the churches of this country. They soon experienced severe culture shock. They had been used to lively services and warm friendly people around them. They soon found that most of the churches they visited were not quite like that. They found, for the most part, that they simply did not fit into the typically British church, and so West Indian churches (and also a few Asian churches) gradually came into being.

One of the first sizeable West Indian denominations to be established in Britain was the Church of God of Prophecy, soon followed by the New Testament Church of God. These two groups still account for a major section of West Indian Christians in Britain. They are very similar in belief and practice. The Church of God of Prophecy split from the New Testament Church of God over certain financial issues some years back. Both churches are strongly charismatic and are headed up by a national overseer. The New Testament Church of God sets out its articles of faith in fourteen different affirmations. Speaking in tongues is regarded as the initial evidence of being baptised in the Holy Spirit, and sanctification is seen as being subsequent to new birth. Baptism is reserved for believers and is in the name of the Trinity and by immersion. These churches place an emphasis on healing as having been provided for in the atoning work of Christ. They also believe in the premillennial second coming of Christ.

Considerable emphasis is placed on holiness in West Indian Pentecostal churches. The implications of this are spelt out in some detail for the benefit of church members. They are required to refrain from the use of alcohol and tobacco, from attendance at cinemas or dance halls, and from mixed bathing, except with the immediate family. Members are forbidden to wear jewellery. In the case of the Church of God of Prophecy even wedding rings are ruled out.

The New Testament Church of God has a training college for candidates for the full-time ministry at Overstone near Northampton. This college is open to other denominations. The international headquarters of the church is at Cleveland,

USA. Although in this country the leadership is in the hands of black Christians this is not the case in other parts of the world.

The government of the church is somewhat similar to Methodism. The United Kingdom is divided into 23 districts, presiding over each of which is a district overseer. Quarterly conferences take place for instruction and mutual encouragement.

In most of the West Indian Pentecostal churches the services are considerably longer than in the average English free church and certainly much more emotionally charged. The exercise of spiritual gifts is encouraged. Women participate in the services, but most of them, particularly the older women, feel it is right to have their heads covered. Foot washing is practised regularly in many of the churches. There is keen interest in missionary work overseas. Ghana, Liberia and Nigeria are amongst those countries to which special attention is given.

In 1961 the New Testament Assembly arrived in Britain, pioneered in the main by two pastors, Melvin Powell and Donald Bernard. Since then its fellowships have grown steadily in numbers, especially in the London area, but also in Leicester and Derby. It now has more than 2,000 members and around fifty ordained ministers and evangelists. The New Testament Assembly was founded in Jamaica in 1954. The church has a concern for evangelism and also to implement the social implications of the gospel. It has sponsored youth clubs and counselling groups and has launced a Christian Concern for the Elderly project. The church is a member of the West Indian Evangelical Alliance.

It is well to bear in mind that denominationally the West Indian Pentecostal churches belong to a quite different tradition from English Pentecostal churches such as Elim or the Assemblies of God. In addition to the larger groups over here there are numerous small denominations as well as totally independent churches.

In 1986 the Bibleway Church of our Lord Jesus Christ

Worldwide celebrated its silver jubilee. It is headed up in Britain by Bishop L E White and its headquarters is at Lewisham in South-East London. Churches have been established in various parts of London as well as in Bedford, Birmingham, Cambridge, Peterborough, Ipswich and Wellingborough. The church claims to be both Pentecostal and Apostolic. It practises foot washing at communion.

The Wesleyan Holiness Church was first established in the United Kingdom in 1958 and operates chiefly in London and the West Midlands. Its form of church government is closely akin to that of Methodism and it is not Pentecostal. It has approximately a thousand members in Britain.

One of the most highly respected leaders among the West Indian Christian community is Philip Mohabir from Guyana, who describes himself as a missionary to Britain. He heads up the West Indian Evangelical Alliance and also has links with the house church movement. Converted from Hinduism, Philip Mohabir was for 19 years engaged in pioneering church work in the Guyanas and Caribbean islands. He now lives with his family in Brixton where half the population is black and the level of unemployment among the highest in Europe. It is Philip Mohabir's dream to link more closely the 3,000 or so black-led churches which are attended by up to 100,000 Christians.

It is an experience to attend a West Indian service. To describe it as lively would be an understatement! There is exuberance and emotion with plenty of congregational participation. The preaching is simple and Bible-based. The pastor is very much a 'father figure' to the congregation. West Indians choose to dress up for church services. Many of the women will wear a hat or scarf. They believe in the exercise of spiritual gifts and openly practise praying for the sick and casting out demons.

In 1976 the Afro/West Indian United Council of Churches was formed, based in Shoreditch in East London. It aims to provide a forum for church leaders to discuss common problems, particularly social and political issues. The council is anxious to break down the insularity often associated with the black-led churches.

Many West Indian church leaders bemoan the fact that they are largely cold-shouldered by the white Christian community. Philip Mohabir explains it in this way: 'We are a more significant Christian force than any other community in the United Kingdom. The churches are growing steadily, but are practically unknown to the host community ... vast sections of the evangelical world do not know that we exist.' There is a growing desire on the part of the West Indian community to build bridges and forge links with white churches.

In speaking of 'black churches' it also ought to be said that there are here and there indigenous white churches in Britain which have succeeded in integrating West Indians into their congregations. It is of course a fact that most of the Afro-Caribbean immigrants who came here settled in the inner cities where few churches have a congregation of any size. Sadly, the few Christians in the community were in the main totally unprepared to receive and accommodate people from a different culture. Lack of cultural sensitivity on both sides contributed to the general feeling of intrusion on the one hand and being unwanted on the other. Christians on the whole seemed unable to cope with the situation, giving up all hope of integrating the new communities into their churches. Thank God there have been some exceptions. It is an interesting fact that four white-led churches opted to join the West Indian Evangelical Alliance.

There are Afro/West Indian sects represented over here which are a departure from orthodox Christianity. One such sect is the Sacred Cherubim and Seraphim Society which has its roots in Lagos. It mingles freely practices derived from several different sources. Leaders of the society are referred to as apostles and prophets. Members of the sect wear white robes and coloured sashes. On entering the church building everyone must remove their footwear and all members cross themselves. Candles and incense are used in worship, and the Bible is read. Speaking in tongues is practised, and much emphasis is placed on dreams and visions. The church represents an amalgam of Catholic and Pentecostal practices combined with a good deal of African cultural and spiritist influences.

When it comes to church growth, the black-led churches in Britain are probably expanding faster than almost any other denomination.

10

The Salvation Army

In 1965 the Salvation Army celebrated its centenary. Its founder, William Booth, a Methodist New Connexion minister, felt an inner compulsion to seek out those out of touch with all organised religion, particularly as he saw them in the East End of London. The Christian Mission which he started has over the years developed into an international movement widely respected throughout the world.

William Booth was born in Nottingham on April 10, 1829, and was converted at the age of 15. When he came to London as a young man, he linked up with what was then known as the Methodist Reform Movement. Later he was invited to take charge of a Methodist circuit in Lincolnshire which was associated with the Reform Movement. Subsequently he offered himself to the Methodist New Connexion and was accepted as a probationary minister in a London circuit. By this time William Booth had proved himself a most successful 'soul winner', and he soon found himself in great demand as a leader of evangelistic campaigns. In 1855 he married Catherine Mumford, an earnest Christian woman.

It was during a period of service in Gateshead that William and Catherine Booth began to think through those principles which were later to lead to the formation of the Salvation Army. In 1861 a Methodist Conference decided that William Booth should be asked to take the position of circuit minister rather than be set free for full-time evangelistic work; he and his wife consequently decided the time had come for them to resign. They soon found themselves in great demand for evangelistic work in many different parts of the country. Nevertheless, they found increasing opposition from the main denominations and were often forced to use secular halls and other public buildings for their meetings.

Mrs Booth, a truly remarkable evangelist, conducted a number of campaigns on her own without the help of her husband, with marked success. It was largely as the outcome of a campaign which she conducted in Rotherhithe in 1865 that the Salvation Army was founded.

The Booths believed that London should be their main target. William Booth felt that he was called to minister to the people of the East End in particular. He had many converts as a result of a tent mission which he conducted in Whitechapel, but he feared that those who had confessed Christ would find it hard to settle down in the recognised churches. Therefore he felt constrained to start the East London Christian Mission, largely to follow up his own evangelistic endeavours.

The work done by the Booths in London met with phenomenal success. Mission halls were opened in a number of different areas, and those who had been converted were encouraged to seek out others. From the outset William Booth sought to organise his efforts with military precision. He believed strongly in the need for the application of business principles to religion. At first he had tried to organise the Christian Mission along Methodist lines, holding an annual conference, but he came to feel that this hampered the progress of the work. He himself took over full control of the mission, the conference continuing only as a council of war.

The Christian Mission magazine of September 1878 stated that the mission had organised 'a Salvation Army to carry the blood of Christ and the power of the Holy Ghost to every corner of the world'. By the end of that year the Salvation Army had replaced the Christian Mission as the name of William Booth's movement, and the general superintendent was henceforth 'the General', the sole director of the work, with power to nominate his successor. Mission stations were now referred to as 'corps', and military titles were adopted for those in charge. Uniforms followed within a matter of two or three years.

During these early years the Army met with fierce opposition. Its attacks, for example, upon the evil of strong drink incurred the wrath of the brewing industry. Many riots and disturbances occurred. Determined efforts were made by hooligans to break up the Army, and many Salvationists were themselves arrested and put into prison.

For all the persecution they suffered, the ardour of the 'soldiers' remained unaffected. As time went on people in high places came to see the value of the work. In 1882, at a time when the Army was still very much under fire, Dr Lightfoot, Bishop of Durham, declared: 'Whatever may be its faults, the Salvation Army has at least recalled us to this lost ideal of the work of the church – the universal compulsion of the souls of men.' That same year an attempt was made to bring the Salvation Army under the aegis of the Church of England, but negotiations broke down and the scheme was eventually dropped. This resulted in the formation in 1882 of the Church Army, an Anglican counterpart to the Salvation Army.

Now that the Army was growing rapidly the General felt it necessary to draw up a clear-cut statement which would-be officers would have to sign. The declaration, known as Articles of War, made stringent demands upon would-be soldiers:

(1) A profession of personal salvation.

(2) A pledge of separation from the world and of loyalty to Jesus Christ.

(3) A pledge of allegiance to the Army to be expressed, among other ways, by obedience to its officers.

(4) An expression of faith in the possibility of holy living.

(5) A pledge of total abstinence from the use of all intoxicating

liquors and baneful drugs.
(6) A promise to devote all leisure time and spare energy and money to help forward the Salvation war.

From the outset one of the features of the Salvation Army has been its insistence that women should enjoy equal rights with men in the work of publishing salvation. After a while women were placed in charge of mission stations. The time came when women found themselves placed in high command, which often involved them in exercising authority over subordinate men officers. The work of the Salvation Army in France and in Sweden was largely pioneered by women. In 1907, Mrs Bramwell Booth, daughter-in-law of the General, inaugurated the Home League, an association of Salvationist women who meet weekly for fellowship and for instruction in better home-building. This movement now has a membership in the British Isles of over 43,700 women.

William Booth realised the need for providing adequate training for young and uninstructed officers. The first large training centre he set up was in Clapton, where a fine building was erected, known as Congress Hall. In 1929 the William Booth Memorial Training College at Denmark Hill was opened.

It was about the year 1880 that the Salvation Army became truly international in character. Today the Army works in eighty-nine countries with over 14,500 evangelistic centres and 2,151 halls, usually referred to as citadels. It is computed that the Army conducts thousands of open-air meetings weekly throughout the year.

Social service has always been an outstanding feature of the Army's work. In 1890 William Booth published his historic volume *In Darkest England and the Way Out*, a book which brought to the notice of the general public much evil of which the average man or woman was ignorant. This book did a great deal to win respect for the Salvation Army. Responsible men and women came to see that Salvationists felt deeply for the outcast and the needy, and were genuinely trying to help them. Almost every one of William Booth's proposals for social welfare as set forth in his book is now an integral part of the Army's work.

Today there are two Salvation Army homes in Great Britain devoted exclusively to the highly specialised and difficult work of training maladjusted children.

In Great Britain the Army provides thirty-five hostels for the homeless, and daily shelter is provided for over 8,000 men and women 'with an unsettled way of life'. From thirty-three goodwill centres in the congested areas of Britain, Salvationists minister to the material as well as the spiritual needs of men and women, giving special attention to the sick and aged, and arranging holidays and outings for tired mothers and their children.

The work of the Missing Persons Bureau is well known. On average, 5,000 inquiries are dealt with each year. In London's King's Cross area, trained Salvation Army women officers patrol the streets during the late hours and seek to offer counsel and help to girls in moral danger. Salvation Army officers engage in prison visitation and are active in helping discharged prisoners to re-establish themselves. There are no less than thirty-seven Eventide homes in Britain where the aged are cared for.

The Army newspaper – the *War Cry* – is widely read among Salvationists. Salvationists take copies into the homes of people when visiting and use it in public houses as a means of spreading the gospel. The Army has its own printing works in St Albans – the Campfield Press – and it issues numerous periodicals serving all the various interests of the movement.

In addition to all this, of course, there is the widespread overseas work of the Army. The Salvation Army claims to preach the gospel in 127 languages and operates 216 hospitals and dispensaries. India was the first field to be entered, but today the Army is active in Pakistan, Burma, Sri Lanka, East and West Africa, South Africa, Indonesia, Malaya, South America, the Caribbean and Hong Kong, as well as numerous other areas.

From the outset music and singing were regarded as of vital importance to the work. Brass bands were introduced with the idea of assisting the singing. No one may be in the band who is not a member of the Army, and all the instruments remain the property of the Army. Much of the Army's best music is the creation of Salvationists. William Booth is credited with having asked, 'Why should the Devil have all the best tunes?', and he encouraged the singing of hymns to popular tunes. The International Music Council is now the recognised authority for regulating the music used by the Salvation Army. At their services hymns are spoken of as 'songs', and are usually accompanied both by the band and also by tambourines wielded by the songsters or choir.

I will mention now a number of other distinctive features of the Salvation Army. Total abstinence from alcohol has always been a condition of membership. The use of conventional mourning is frowned upon in Salvation Army circles as being opposed to the teaching of Christ. The General introduced the Cross and Crown badge to be worn on the left arm by those bereaved – this being regarded as a mark of respect for the departed. The children of Salvationists are not baptised but are dedicated at a devotional service. Candidates for soldiership publicly profess their faith in the Lord Jesus Christ, declare their separation from the world, its sins and its pleasures, and pledge their entire devotion to the service of Christ.

William Booth was convinced that the sacraments were to be regarded as symbols of spiritual truth and that Christian people should be primarily concerned to seek the experience which such symbols represented. He called upon his soldiers to realise that their spiritual life was dependent upon constant recognition of their union with Christ as their Saviour, and he claimed that 'at every meal they should remember that Christ's body was broken for their salvation'. For these reasons, Salvationists do not have services of baptism or Holy Communion.

Self-denial has always been strongly emphasised in the Salvation Army, and annually a self-denial week is held when an appeal is made, not only to the Salvationists, but to the public generally, for support for the work.

The distinctive uniform of the Salvationists has been regarded as a means of witnessing for Christ and as an outward sign of separation from the world. Although, as a body, Salvationists are a joyous people, nevertheless they voluntarily submit to a rigid discipline hardly comparable with anything found in any other section of the Christian church. Their officers rarely stay longer than three or four years in one appointment, and they have to be ready to be sent to any part of the world at very short notice.

The Army boasts, with justification, that it serves on every front. Not only in time of war, but also under normal conditions, members of the Forces are welcomed into Red Shield canteens. In times of national emergency and disaster the Salvation Army is often one of the first organisations to be on the scene. The work of the Army is admired by many who make no religious profession at all, and even supported by them. The Army, incidentally, is quite uninhibited in seeking financial support from any who are prepared to give it.

In certain respects, the Salvation Army as we know it today is very different from its early beginnings. It set out to reach the outcasts of society, but in many a citadel today the congregation is made up of similar people to those found in the average church. Some would criticise the Army on the grounds that its social work tends sometimes to predominate over its spiritual activities. Undoubtedly William Booth had a deep concern to minister both to men's souls and bodies, and it is still true that Salvationists generally share that concern. Some would feel that the training of the Salvation Army officers is inadequate from the theological point of view, and that many who occupy positions of leadership have not been sufficiently rooted and grounded in the faith. There is inevitably a certain danger along this line in a movement where such a strong emphasis is placed upon experience and enthusiasm.

Many churchmen, of course, find it hard to appreciate the

attitude of William Booth, and indeed the Salvation Army generally, towards the sacraments. There is perhaps a growing number of Salvationists who themselves feel a lack in this direction, and who from time to time attend churches of different denominations for the purpose of sharing in the Lord's Supper.

In recent years the Army has become less insular and has been ready to join in inter-church activities. Certainly at many united services the Salvation Army band is much in evidence, and Salvation Army officers are frequently invited to join ministers' fraternals. The Army is a member of the Evangelical Alliance.

The Army has always had its critics. It has often been accused of begging. Some have been critical on theological grounds, particularly those who have pronounced views regarding the electing grace of God and who, on scriptural grounds, argue strongly against the contention that a person once saved may nevertheless subsequently be lost should they fall again into sinful ways – a view held by the Army. Yet, for all the criticisms Christian people generally are generous in the tribute they pay not only to 'the General', but to the Army which he recruited and led, and which continues to this day to 'wage a good warfare'.

11

Christian Brethren

Christian Brethren are to be found all over the world, although often the name 'Christian Brethren' does not appear on notice boards or in their literature. The movement began between the years 1825 and 1830, and initially it took root in Dublin, Plymouth and Bristol. The meeting in Plymouth quickly grew to a membership of over one thousand which accounts for the nickname 'Plymouth' Brethren. Many Christian Brethren today take exception to being referred to as 'Plymouth' Brethren.

The man who might well be regarded as the founder of the movement was John Nelson Darby (1819–82) who had studied at Trinity College, Dublin, and was later ordained as a minister of the Church of England in Ireland. Darby was joined by Anthony Norris Groves, a dentist and missionary in Baghdad and India; Samuel Prideaux Tregelles, the eminent New Testament textual critic; and George Müller, who founded the famous orphan homes in Bristol.

The early Brethren were primarily concerned for the church to return to the teachings of Scripture, not only as regards such matters as personal salvation and conduct, but also as regards simplicity of worship. They claimed that, as disciples of Christ, they were free to 'break bread' with any of the Lord's people, and they believed that they were following scriptural practice in meeting for this purpose every Lord's Day.

The position taken up by the Brethren was put very clearly by A N Groves: 'Our aim is that men should come together in all simplicity as disciples, not waiting on any pulpit or ministry but trusting that the Lord will edify us together by ministering to us, as he sees good for ourselves.' From the outset the emphasis of the Brethren has been placed emphatically on the priesthood of all believers. They repudiated any and every form of clericalism and stressed that, in the local assembly, those called to leadership must be guided by the Holy Spirit.

From the earliest days prominence was given to the doctrine of Christ's personal return. J N Darby was responsible for a prodigious amount of work, and he succeeded in the midst of his pastoral activities and his travels abroad in translating the whole Bible into French, as well as making a new English translation. In some parts of the world the Brethren are still referred to as Darbyists.

Unfortunately, in 1849 there was a serious split in the ranks of the Brethren. This led to the formation of the two main groups often referred to nowadays as Open Brethren and Exclusive (or Close) Brethren. The point at issue largely concerned the doctrinal soundness of B W Newton, the leader of the Brethren in Plymouth, who had been accused of heresy. It was alleged that he was guilty of erroneous doctrine concerning the humanity of our Lord. He later retracted certain elements in his teaching, but his disclaimer was never accepted by Darby. Furthermore, Newton did not subscribe to Darby's interpretation of prophecy. Newton withdrew from the original meeting place in Plymouth and set up another assembly, later becoming an independent minister in London. In Bethesda Chapel, Bristol, where the leadership was in the hands of George Müller, brother-in-law of A N Groves, a welcome was given to a group who had sat under Newton's ministry in Plymouth. Müller and his colleague Henry Craik were accused of receiving 'unsound' men, and the assembly at Bethesda was condemned for its 'neutrality to Christ'. It was contended by Darby and his followers that he who does not actively condemn error is guilty of it.

The split that occurred at this time has never been healed and to this day there is little, if any, fraternisation between the Open and the Exclusive Brethren. The Open Brethren have consistently stood for the receiving of Christians from other branches of the Christian church to the Lord's Table and having fellowship with them. The Exclusive Brethren (who, incidentally, have had several splits within their own ranks) have always maintained that they only receive those who have come from assemblies of their own persuasion or can prove that they have had no fellowship with error.

It is almost impossible to assess the numerical strength of the Brethren movement in Britain today. It is generally estimated to be upwards of 60,000 as far as the Open Brethren are concerned. In the main body of the Exclusive Brethren there are probably less than 10,000, a large number of whom dissociated from the main body a few years ago. The Open Brethren are particularly strong in Clydeside, Belfast and in the Cardiff area, as well as in London and the Home Counties; and are weakest in rural areas, except for East Anglia, Devon and Somerset. In proportion to the size of the movement there are probably more missionaries drawn from Brethren assemblies than from any other section of the Protestant Church in Britain. Brethren missionary work is registered as Christian Missions in Many Lands. In addition to those working 'on faith lines' in association with the assemblies, others are serving with different interdenominational societies. The missionary magazine, *Echoes of Service*, with its headquarters in Bath, gives news of the activities of Brethren missionaries and channels funds that are sent from the different assemblies for their support, although much of this is sent directly from local assemblies to the missionaries concerned.

I will look now at some of the main features of the Brethren movement. Doctrinally, the Brethren accept the position often referred to in these days as 'conservative evangelical'. The Bible is their 'only infallible rule of faith and practice'. The Open Brethren adhere strongly to believers' baptism by immersion on personal confession of faith. They do not, however, demand baptism as a condition for partaking of the Lord's Supper. They receive, at the Lord's Table, all believers known to be sound in faith and godly in life, but they do in some assemblies require that they shall bring a letter of introduction or be commended by a local Christian friend known to the assembly. Meetings for worship are regarded as being strictly under the guidance of the Holy Spirit, and opportunity is given for any present to take part. Anyone is free to announce a hymn, to read a portion of Scripture, or to pass on a message from the word of God.

A group of elders, sometimes referred to as the oversight (from 1 Peter 5:2), watch over the spiritual interests of the local assembly. The procedure whereby they are appointed varies.

Brethren lay great stress on the breaking of bread service. When those who have been brought up in the assemblies gravitate towards some other section of the Christian church they usually say that the one thing that they miss most is the service of breaking of bread. The service itself is marked by the utmost simplicity. A loaf is used and passed from seat to seat among the assembled company, each communicant breaking a morsel of bread from the loaf. The common cup is used and this too is passed from worshipper to worshipper. Different brethren give thanks for the bread and the wine prior to the actual breaking of bread. In recent years there has been a growing practice among Christian Brethren of holding the breaking of bread service at an earlier hour in the morning and following this at 11 or 11.30 by a preaching service, much on the lines of the free churches. This practice is very common among Brethren in the United States. The evening service, usually called the Gospel Service, is, as its name implies, evangelistic in purpose. Either a visiting speaker or members of the local assembly conduct the service.

There is a growing tendency to recognise certain men as being set apart for full-time Christian service among the assemblies, although not necessarily to the pastoral care of any one church. In the post-war years there has been much

thought among the Brethren concerning their spiritual effectiveness, and conferences have been held at which time has
been given to the consideration of Brethren principles and
practice. Particular concern has been expressed for the training of young men to serve among the Brethren assemblies. An
annual conference has been held for the past few years at
Swanwick, attended by upwards of 300 people, at which
responsible leaders have given instruction in Christian doctrine and other matters.

One could say regarding the Brethren that there is a
minimum of organisation and a maximum of elasticity. Each
local church is autonomous, and there is considerable varia-
tion between different churches, or 'assemblies' as they are
usually called. There are relatively few assemblies of great
numerical strength – the average assembly numbers less than
100 members.

Although, as we have pointed out, elders are normally
appointed, no one elder is commissioned necessarily to take
the lead. Thus, any elder may administer baptism or conduct a
wedding or a funeral. This liberty, of course, has its draw-
backs. There are occasions of embarrassment in Brethren
assemblies when those who are perhaps less fitted tend to
dominate the scene. Such occasions, however, are happily
rare. The whole Brethren concept of the church calls for a
high degree of spirituality.

Over the years the Brethren movement has attracted to
itself some outstanding business and professional men, and on
the whole it has probably appealed to the middle and professional classes more than to other sections of the community.
Brethren as a whole do not look with favour upon the ecumenical movement, although there are instances where Brethren
assemblies take a full share in the work of a local council of
churches. Open Brethren are usually very ready to co-operate
in interdenominational activities which are truly evangelical in
character. It has been computed that at the Billy Graham
Crusades held in Britain, over 25% of the counsellors were
recruited from the ranks of the Christian Brethren. They have

also played a particularly active part in a number of inter-denominational youth movements, such as Covenanters (founded by Brethren) and Crusaders, and many of them have shown an active interest and participation in the establishment of the London Bible College. Their influence in the evangelical world generally is out of all proportion to their numerical strength. Over the years they have produced some outstanding Bible teachers and evangelists and from time to time have taken an active part in the ministry of the word at such gatherings as the Keswick Convention.

There are one or two features of Brethren meetings that perhaps ought to be mentioned. Traditionally women have taken a far less vocal part than they do in most of the free churches. Brethren are particularly sensitive to the teaching of the apostle Paul on these matters. Women in some assemblies are not encouraged to take part in prayer at prayer meetings when both men and women are present, and neither are they allowed to preach or speak at gatherings when both sexes are participating. It used not to be customary at the morning meeting for an organ or other instrument to be used. There is a tendencey, however, for these traditions to be broken nowadays.

Many young men and women, particularly those going to university, tend to leave the Brethren and align themselves with some other branch of the Christian church. This may be partly due to the fact that their eyes are opened to other – and for some more appealing – forms of worship, as well as to the value of consecutive biblical ministry. It is interesting to note that when young people and even older folk leave the assemblies for some other branch of the Christian church, they tend to turn towards the Church of England rather than the free churches (although it is also true that some of the 'pillars' in nonconformist churches were recruited from those formerly associated with the Brethren). That so many opt for the Church of England may possibly be explained by the fact that, like the Brethren, Anglicans emphasise the importance of the Lord's Supper. It could be said of Brethren assemblies that they fall mainly into two categories: those that are open to change, and those dying a slow lingering death. To the dismay of some the more radical assemblies have a habit of glossing over their background and ceasing to regard themselves as Christian Brethren.

What of the Exclusive Brethren? As the very designation implies, those who belong to this group keep themselves very much to themselves, and it is virtually impossible to get any reliable information or statistics about them. They did, however, attract public notice some years ago following a pronouncement made by one of their leaders in America regarding the need for separation from all worldly associations on the part of church members. This principle has been applied so rigidly that even within a household those who are not 'in fellowship' are forbidden to eat at the same time as those who are. Furthermore, students have been told that they should not take their degrees, and members of professional bodies have been told it is their duty to resign from such membership.

This pronouncement did, in fact, cause a major split within the Exclusive ranks. Many who had been brought up among the Exclusives (one estimate puts the number at over 6,000) severed their connection completely and sought fellowship in other branches of the Christian church, although they did not for the most part join up with the Open Brethren, whom they had been brought up to regard as being beyond the pale! Some formed new assemblies of their own, but most of these have now ceased to exist.

Among the Exclusives there are a number of groups which are less rigid than the rest. The largest and perhaps most exclusive group is often referred to as the London Party. The Glanton Brethren are probably the least exclusive of the Exclusives, and the Kelly Brethren likewise are far less rigid than the London Party. One interesting feature of the Exclusive Brethren is that most groups are paedobaptist – they practise the household baptism of infants.

Returning now to the Open Brethren, certain emphases have traditionally been associated with them, particularly regarding prophecy. While all have a very real interest in the subject of the Lord's return, probably a majority would subscribe to a particular interpretation of prophecy, usually referred to as dispensationalism. This view finds expression in the notes of the Scofield Bible, which has been widely followed in Brethren circles. It would be true to say, however, that a growing number of Brethren do not accept this particular viewpoint, at least not in every detail. There have, in fact, always been men in the ranks of the Brethren who have dissented from it – for example, George Müller, Dan Crawford and Robert Chapman.

Assemblies in Scotland and Northern Ireland tend to be less open to change than in other parts. Amongst the Christian Brethren as a whole there are two distinct strands – the Traditionalists and the Progressives. While the Traditionalists are reluctant to see any changes, the Progressives have in many cases countenanced the appointment of full-time workers – some are actually referred to as 'ministers'. The Gospel Hall has become the Evangelical Church, and women are no longer required to wear hats and are encouraged to participate in open worship. Whereas the Traditionalists would set their faces sternly against any activities which would be remotely described as charismatic, the Progressive assemblies rejoice in the worship songs and choruses so popular in many churches today. Much of the progressive thinking in Brethren circles today stems from the activities of the Christian Brethren Research Fellowship, founded in 1963 and dedicated to research projects and seminars concerning matters affecting Christian Brethren churches in the United Kingdom and overseas.

The Harvester, widely read in Brethren circles, gives particulars of Brethren activities, together with general articles on Christian doctrine and practice which are often very thought-provoking. *The Harvester* is read and enjoyed by a much wider circle than the Brethren themselves.

In conclusion it should be said that the whole evangelical world owes an incalculable debt to the Christian Brethren.

They have, for the most part, entered wholeheartedly into many interdenominational activities. Perhaps Christian youth movements owe the greatest debt of all to them. The evangelistic enthusiasm of the Brethren is a challenge to Christians generally, and the scale of their missionary activities is out of all proportion to their numerical strength. Like all branches of the Christian church they have their limitations and their weaknesses, the most noticeable of which has perhaps been an inclination in certain cases to engage in theological hair splitting over relatively unimportant details.

The Open Brethren have been preserved from the divisions which have characterised the Exclusives, largely because of their firm adherence to the principle of the autonomy of the local church. It is praiseworthy that the Brethren themselves appear to be increasingly conscious of their shortcomings and willing to face up to them. In any case, no one familiar with the history of any one of the denominations is in a position to 'cast the first stone'.

12

The Pentecostalists and the Holiness Movement

At various points in the history of the church, groups have emerged which might loosely be described as 'charismatic' – Christians who reacted against institutionalism and sought a more free type of spiritual expression, with emphasis on spiritual gifts.

In the second century, the Montanists claimed that all the gifts of the Spirit were still operative in the church. Although many of them went to extremes they could number among them a church leader of outstanding quality, Tertullian, and one of the most heroic of Christian martyrs, Perpetua.

Centuries passed with little or no reference to spiritual gifts. It was generally assumed that the gifts had been specifically given for the founding of the church, and had been subsequently withdrawn when they seemed no longer necessary. However, there were times of spiritual awakening when charismatic manifestations were again evident. It is claimed, for instance, that Martin Luther 'was endowed with all the gifts of the Spirit'. Some of the early Quakers 'spoke in tongues'. It was, however, during the nineteenth century, largely through the influence of Edward Irving, that the subject of spiritual gifts again came to the fore. Ordained as a minister in the Church of Scotland, Irving later came to London where he preached to great crowds. He contended that the spiritual gifts of the apostolic age were a permanent endowment of the church, restrained only by the unbelief of Christians. Members of his congregation spoke in tongues and miraculous healings took place. Irving combined fervent belief in the exercise of the gifts with extreme ritualism. He founded the Catholic Apostolic Church which is now virtually extinct.

The modern Pentecostal movement may be traced back to extraordinary spiritual manifestations which took place at 312 Azusa Street, Los Angeles, in the year 1906. Here was the site of a run-down Methodist mission. It was visited by a Negro preacher, W J Seymour, who proclaimed that anyone who does not speak in tongues is not baptised with the Holy Spirit. For three years without a break, prayer meetings were held at 312 Azusa Street with speaking in tongues, singing in the Spirit and prophecy. The movement soon spread, not only to other parts of America but also to Britain. Many of the early Pentecostalists were children of the Welsh revival which had reached its peak in 1904. The Rev A A Boddy, an Anglican clergyman who had taken part in the revival, is often referred to as the father of the British Pentecostal movement. He was vicar of All Saints' Church in Sunderland, and his parish hall became a centre for those seeking the experience of 'the baptism of the Spirit'.

Early in 1907, Boddy visited Oslo where he met Mr T B Barrett, an Englishman who headed up the city mission there. Barrett had experienced 'baptism in the Spirit' when he visited America. Boddy was greatly impressed by this man and invited him to visit his church in Sunderland. Mr Boddy attended the Keswick Convention of 1907 and distributed a pamphlet entitled 'Pentecost for England'. In it he wrote, 'It is said that 20,000 people today are speaking with tongues, or have so spoken…yet not more than perhaps half a dozen persons are known by the writer to have had this experience in Great Britain.'

In September 1907 T B Barrett, a former Methodist minister, arrived in England and for several weeks preached the message of Pentecost in the parish hall of All Saints' Church in Sunderland. A steady stream of Christians attended from varied denominational backgrounds, and it was said, 'the eyes of the religious millions of Great Britain are now fixed upon Sunderland'. One person who attended was Smith Wigglesworth, then leader of Bowland Street Mission in Bradford.

Wigglesworth's personal Pentecost had far-reaching effects. He was to become an outstanding influence in the Pentecostal movement, not only in Britain but throughout the world. The year 1907 witnessed a remarkable spread of the movement simultaneously in widely separated parts of the world – in Scandinavia, in Holland and in India, as well as throughout the British Isles. In January 1909, a meeting was held in All Saints' Vicarage, Sunderland, which led to the formation of the Pentecostal Missionary Union. This, in 1925, merged with the Assemblies of God (see below). Mr Cecil Polhill, one of the famous 'Cambridge Seven', was elected president. He and Mr Boddy were the most outstanding figures in the formative years of the Pentecostal movement in Britain. It is noteworthy that the movement began within the Anglican Church and that its early leaders were staunch Anglicans, remaining so to the end of their lives. In those days there was no encouragement given to the forming of separate Pentecostal fellowships. The counsel usually given was to 'receive the baptism in the Holy Spirit, but remain in your church, whatever the denomination may be'.

It is hardly surprising that with the passage of time the 'old wineskins' proved incapable of containing the 'new wine'. Donald Gee in his book *The Pentecostal Movement* comments that 'for many precious years the movement floundered for lack of strong, inspiring, distinctive leadership'. It suffered, too, from the activities of the extremists, the 'lunatic fringe' that brought it into disrepute. Some greatly respected Christian leaders strongly opposed the movement, while others greeted it with indifference or even ridicule. Out of the movement emerged two outstanding evangelists – the Jeffreys brothers, Stephen and George – and it is largely through their desire to have an organisation behind them that the Elim Church eventually came into being as a distinct denomination. Donald Gee makes the comment that one of the reasons for the formation of Pentecostal denominations was to protect the movement from 'worthless religious tramps'. He adds: 'The amazing freedom of the meetings gave opportunity for undesirables to take advantage for personal ends.' The Apostolic Church with its roots in Wales was one of the earliest Pentecostal denominations to be formed. Its first leader was Dan P Williams of Penygroes, South Wales, and its headquarters are still located there. The Apostolic Church claims to possess a 'fuller vision' regarding church order, and it emphasises the place of the prophetic ministry. It believes in the office of apostle and believes that today's apostles have 'authority to loose, authority to bind, authority to excommunicate, authority to re-admit, authority to establish churches'.

The Elim Four Square Alliance, as it was originally known, took shape in 1926 with the intention that it should become an umbrella organisation for all Pentecostals in Great Britain. However this was not to be. The term 'four square' was used to express the four dominant notes of the message, namely that the Lord Jesus is Saviour, Healer, Baptiser in the Holy Spirit and Coming King. The Elim Pentecostal Church adopted a centralised, presbyterian form of church government. On the other hand, the Assemblies of God, which were constituted in 1924, adopted a congregational form of government. They stress that 'speaking in tongues is the scriptural initial evidence of the baptism in the Holy Spirit' and refuse to accept that so-called Pentecostal experiences without such an outward and physical manifestation are valid. In the years 1930 to 1935 the Pentecostal movement in Great Britain saw considerable growth, largely through successful evangelistic campaigns which always included an emphasis upon healing. This was followed by a period of consolidation when stress was placed on the ministry of teaching and upon the pastoral office. Since then the Pentecostal denominations have tended to become increasingly 'respectable' and have been welcomed into the membership of such bodies as the Evangelical Alliance. It could be said that something of the fire which characterised the movement in its early days is no longer so noticeable. To some extent the Pentecostal denominations have 'settled down'. Looking at it from another angle one could say the traditional Pentecostalists have been overtaken by the renewal movement, sometimes referred to as neo-Pentecostalism.

The various Pentecostal 'denominations' are well organised. The Elim Church has its headquarters in Cheltenham and a very fine Bible College located at Nantwich in Cheshire. There are about 380 Elim churches in existence and some 26,000 members. The church's International Missions Department supports work in several European countries, in different parts of Africa, and in Guyana, Hong Kong and India.

The Assemblies of God headquarters is in Nottingham, with a Bible College at Mattersey in Yorkshire. The denomination shows a keen interest in work overseas and is active in Europe and Africa, as well as in Papua New Guinea, Taiwan and Malaysia. There are some 60,000 church members in Britain served by over 700 pastors.

The Apostolic Church is considerably smaller, with less than 5,000 members. Oversight of local churches is carried out by recognised apostles and prophets. Missionary work is carried out in several African countries, as well as in Europe and Brazil.

In addition to these three main groups there are a number of Pentecostal churches which remain entirely independent.

Worship in a Pentecostal church is usually considered more lively than in the average free church. Members of the congregation are encouraged to participate in worship in which singing plays a prominent part. Opportunity is given for the exercise of such spiritual gifts as speaking in tongues or giving a word of prophecy. Prayers for healing may also be included.

Recent years have witnessed a remarkable growth pattern

in Pentecostal churches. The annual conferences of both the Elim churches and the Assemblies of God bring together over 6,000 people. Churches have been recapturing the spirit which characterised the early years of the movement. One of the largest congregations in London meets in Kensington Temple where two services are held every Sunday morning. Pentecostal leaders take their place in such movements as the Evangelical Alliance, Scripture Union and CARE Trust, and have given their support to evangelists such as Billy Graham and Luis Palau. There is a resurgence of interest in 'reformed theology' in some Pentecostal circles and biblical scholarship is no longer frowned upon.

Pentecostal leaders would be the first to admit their disappointment that, generally speaking, their efforts to touch the working classes have not been successful. They do display increasing social concern for the more needy members of the community. They run rehabilitation centres for alcoholics and drug addicts and are seeking to tackle the problems of the 'inner city'. Like most denominations, the Pentecostalists have their extremists, but as a whole Pentecostal churches relate happily to other fellowships which, like them, are Bible-based.

The Holiness Movement, although quite distinct from Pentecostalism, has certain affinities with it. This began in the British Isles with the Rev George Sharpe, a Congregational minister who was dismissed from his charge in Parkhead, Glasgow, for preaching 'scriptural holiness'. The first Holiness church started meeting in 1906 in the Great Eastern Road Halls, Glasgow. Other churches were subsequently formed and they united with the Church of the Nazarene, a 'holiness' church of American origin, in November 1915. In Battersea, London, the International Holiness Mission was started in 1907 by a Mr David Thomas, and this also united with the Church of the Nazarene in 1952. This union brought a further twenty-eight churches, with over 1,000 members and many more adherents, into the Church of the Nazarene.

Yet another Holiness group, known as the Calvary Holiness Church, united with the Church of the Nazarene in 1955. It was led by the Rev Maynard G James and the Rev Jack Ford.

The Nazarene college at Didsbury, Manchester, caters for students training for the ministry. In all, there are now approximately 100 churches in Britain belonging to the Church of the Nazarene.

The distinctive emphasis of the Holiness Movement is that in the Atonement the Lord Jesus Christ has made provision not only to save men from their sins but also to 'perfect them in love'. 'We believe that entire sanctification is that act of God, subsequent to regeneration, by which believers are made free from original sin, or depravity, and brought into a state of entire devotement to God, and the holy obedience of love made perfect....'

'Entire sanctification is provided by the blood of Jesus, is wrought instantaneously by faith, preceded by entire consecration; and to this work and state of grace the Holy Spirit bears witness.'

Historically this doctrine has been referred to by a variety of phrases, such as Christian perfection, perfect love, the baptism with the Holy Spirit and Christian 'holiness'. The doctrine is closely akin to that propounded by John Wesley under the name 'perfect love'.

Both in Pentecostalism and in the Holiness Movement the attention of Christians is drawn to the work of the Holy Spirit. Christians generally have to admit that he has been all too often the 'most neglected Person of the Trinity'. It is, however, encouraging to know that now in all denominations a much greater emphasis is placed on the Person and work of the Holy Spirit.

13

Independent Churches and City Missions

Quite apart from those churches linked with the main denominations in Britain, there still remain a large number of local churches and chapels which are entirely independent. Many, but by no means all, of these are affiliated to the FIEC – the Fellowship of Independent Evangelical Churches.

The Fellowship came into being in 1922. Those who formed it were men of strong evangelical convictions who believed that the spiritual unity existing among those of 'like precious faith' should be expressed in practical fellowship and witness. Some held the view that denominationalism as such was contrary to New Testament teaching, while others felt that none of the existing denominations were any longer thoroughly evangelical, and therefore they could not conscientiously associate themselves with any. There were in different parts of the country a number of causes existing entirely independent of one another. Some were designated 'free churches' and others 'Missions', but all were made up of 'Bible-believing' Christians. The FIEC has succeeded in linking many of these together. The condition of membership is not how the churches are organised or the mode in which sacraments are observed, but adherence to a clearly-worded basis of faith and independence of denominational affiliations. Member churches retain their complete autonomy as far as local church government is concerned, but are required to subscribe annually to the doctrinal basis of the Fellowship. Today there are about 450 churches linked together in Britain in this way. The Fellowship also has a considerable number of personal members. Each year an assembly is held in London or in the provinces. At this gathering the president takes office for the ensuing year and a council of management is elected, together with various committees which are responsible for different sections of the work. Churches throughout the country are grouped in territorial auxiliaries in which closer fellowship is enjoyed through such activities as ministers' fraternals and local rallies. Young people's groups in the churches are linked together through the Ambassador Youth Fellowship, and house parties and other activities are organised for the young people. The magazine *Fellowship* circulates among the churches of the Fellowship.

As an incorporated body the FIEC is empowered to accept the trusteeship of church property. The Fellowship plans its own Sunday school lesson courses and annual Scripture examination. Ministers' conferences are also held from time to time. In its early days the Fellowship was sometimes criticised for giving recognition to ministers who, it would seem, were not always adequately trained or equipped for their task. In recent years, however, the tendency has been to tighten up the regulations considerably, with the result that the standard of ministry in the churches linked with the Fellowship has been raised considerably.

Undoubtedly the Fellowship owes more to the late Rev E J Poole-Connor than to any other one individual. It was through his vision that the Fellowship came into being, and to the end he maintained a very decisive influence in its affairs. Although the FIEC has resolutely sought to avoid becoming another denomination, by the very nature of things it inevitably tends to develop in that direction. The Fellowship as a whole maintains a critical attitude towards the ecumenical movement, and there are some in its ranks who would incline towards the rather extreme position taken up by the International Council of Christian Churches who actively oppose organisations like the World Council of Churches – but this would not be true of the majority.

A few years ago the Peculiar People, representing a group of churches with a very interesting history, became associated with the FIEC. The two bodies agreed to work together where possible in fraternal co-operation in the proclamation of the gospel and the defence of evangelical truth. Originally the Peculiar People were a rather exclusive and tightly-knit evangelical community. When this designation became the subject of increasing misunderstanding the title was changed by general consent to Union of Evangelical Churches. They trace their history back to 1834 to a Church of England clergyman named Atkin, who, having been 'baptised with the Holy Spirit', left his church in favour of an itinerant ministry. Through his preaching two Wesleyan local preachers, William Bridges and James Banyard, entered into a similar spiritual experience. Cottage meetings were started, mainly in different parts of Essex, and in due time a commodious chapel was built in Bath Street in South-East London. Those who associated themselves with this new movement were fervently evangelical in their doctrinal position and outlook. They practised the baptism of believers upon confession of faith – the mode of baptism being either by sprinkling or immersion according to the conviction or preference of the individual concerned.

Services of Holy Communion have always been open to all believers. Divine healing with public or private laying-on of hands and the anointing of oil is also practised, although special healing services as such are not held. The practice is still recognised within this community, although probably to a lesser degree than in former days. James Banyard outlined the principles of the group thus: 'We will accept no money for preaching; make no laws; have no book of rules but the Word of God alone. Unless one knows that his sins are forgiven and that his name is in the Lamb's Book of Life we will not accept him as a member of the Church of God.'

With the passing of time, however, a certain number of rules and regulations did become necessary. In 1852 several of the leaders laid hands upon one another, ordaining bishops. In 1865, a council of elders was formed. A trust deed was drawn up in 1906 whereby churches were arranged in circuits for purposes of mutual aid and encouragement, although locally governed and assisted by a committee elected by the church. There has always been a strong emphasis upon youth work in the denomination. Although in the early days the Peculiar People were very much apart from the mainstream of church life, in more recent years these churches have joined enthusiastically in united evangelistic campaigns and have supported conventions and similar gatherings. Most of their churches are still confined to the county of Essex.

The Fellowship of Independent Evangelical Churches is a member of the British Evangelical Council which is a rallying point for those churches which are evangelical and believe strongly that the only real basis for unity is to be found in a common understanding of the gospel. Within the FIEC constituency there are wide divergences of view on secondary issues. There are Grace Baptist churches which believe in particular redemption and restrict communion to believers' baptised by immersion. There are some churches which practise infant baptism. Some are presbyterian in church government, others congregational. The Apostolic Church, the smallest of the three traditional Pentecostal denominations, is a member of the BEC as is the Evangelical Fellowship of Congregational Churches, a conservative group which retained their evangelical identity when the former Congregational denomination became part of the United Reformed Church. Overall the purpose of the BEC is to work for ways of expressing genuine evangelical church unity while remaining separate from doctrinally mixed denominations.

No survey of church life in Britain would be complete without reference to the many City or Town Missions which exist in different parts of the country. Many of these owe their origins to the vision of David Nasmith. He founded a City Mission in his native Glasgow in 1826 which is still in existence today. He later turned his attention to Northern Ireland where he was instrumental in founding the Belfast City Mission which has some twenty missionaries on its staff. In 1835 he came to London and, with the support of two of his friends, he founded the London City Mission whch employs today over 100 missionaries and a score of voluntary evangelists. Nasmith saw these missions as being a handmaid to the churches in evangelising densely populated areas. Other City Missions are to be found in Manchester, Birmingham, Liverpool, Leeds, Bristol, Edinburgh, Dublin and Newcastle.

In most cases these missions concentrate on evangelism through house-to-house visitation and open-air work. In some cases there are mission halls which function very much akin to local free churches. Almost all the City Missions are interdenominational in character. David Nasmith, who died before he reached his fortieth birthday, was instrumental in establishing no less than fifty City Missions, many of which are still in existence.

Charles Booth, in his *Life and Labour in London*, comments that in the 1890s, 'In the poorer parts especially, in almost every street, there is a mission; they are more numerous than schools or churches, and only less numerous than public houses.' Often these missions owed their origin to a group of individuals, or sometimes to a single person. Some existed in most unpretentious premises, but the larger missions often boasted a large central hall with commodious ancillary buildings. Over the years these missions have faced varying fortunes. Some exist to this day, and flourish. Others have long since ceased to exist. Among those still flourishing we could mention Missions linked with the Shaftesbury Society, the Field Lane Foundation (founded in 1841), the Bermondsey and Brook Lane Medical Mission and the Tower Hamlets Mission (which had as its first Superintendent Fred Charrington, a member of the firm of brewers). Some of these missions were the direct outcome of the evangelistic campaigns of Moody and Sankey. There are also a number of medical missions still in existence, although following the National Health Act the character of these has changed somewhat. Some of the public schools, as well as Oxford and Cambridge Universities, are responsible for missions in London and elsewhere.

It is quite impossible to give an adequate and complete picture of church life in Britain because there are so many unattached churches and chapels which have no link with a recognised denominational group, nor with such a body as the Fellowship of Independent Evangelical Churches. Some of these churches have a most interesting history and a large membership. In some cases these churches were at one time associated with one or other of the denominations, but withdrew when 'liberal' theology became more and more predominant. Surrey Chapel, Norwich, affiliated with the FIEC, will always be associated with the great ministries of Robert Govett and D M Panton who served there as pastors for a great many years. In this chapel the ordinance of foot-washing was practised for many years. Charlotte Baptist Chapel, Edinburgh, probably Scotland's outstanding 'independent' church, has always stood for a teaching ministry and has a membership of over 1,000.

It might well be asked, why are so many different churches existing largely in independence of one another? There is no easy explanation. While it could be conceded that in some cases churches sprang into being around a powerful personality with strongly individualistic traits, nevertheless it is also true that many of these independent evangelical churches would never have been formed had not organised nonconformity departed to a large extent from its original doctrinal position. While some evangelical Christians believe that they should stand their ground within their denomination, others feel that they can no longer be associated with a denomination when many of its official spokesmen speak in a way of which they do not approve. Here, then, are the Separatists of the twentieth century, and, while not all will agree with the position that they hold, we must nevertheless recognise the sincerity of those who adhere to that position, often at no small cost to themselves. Generally speaking, those ministers who serve in these independent churches lack even the slender financial 'security' which is offered to their brethren in the main denominations. There is no machinery comparable for example to the moderatorial system in Presbyterianism to facilitate change of pastorates. There have been, and perhaps still are, a few cynics who refer to such a group as the FIEC as a 'Cave of Adullam', but that is an unfair comment. The vast majority of men who serve in such churches do so because of personal convictions, and for no other reason. No group is without its 'misfits' and its extremists, but by and large those who serve in these independent churches and missions are genuinely seeking to make a positive contribution to the cause of evangelism in Britain today.

14

The House Churches

It was during the 1970s that the so-called house church move-ment really got going. Groups of Christians who had been 'baptised in the Spirit' became frustrated by the inflexibility and formalism in many denominational churches. They started meeting together in each other's homes, then later, as numbers grew, they met in hired halls. The 'house church movement' is a loose umbrella title covering a variety of in-dependent charismatic groups which are not linked with any historic denomination – few of them, in fact, meet in houses. In some cases they started by being a splinter group from a local church, while others represent an existing church which has so changed its structure and ways of worship that it could now be loosely described as 'house church'. The house church movement is not all of a piece. Different strands are discern-ible in it.

The strongest of the groups is probably that hitherto associated with Church House in Bradford. It represents a highly organised national network whose leaders form a hierarchy and local churches submit to their authority. They have tended to buy up redundant local churches, and they place a strong emphasis on church discipline and submission to leadership. Under their auspices thousands of people meet each year at various spiritual 'jamborees' throughout the summer months. The group produces a glossy magazine

Restoration, and publishes from time to time a selection of new Christian worship songs. Leaders in this group include Bryn Jones, a Welsh Pentecostalist, Tony Morton, and Terry Virgo, a London Bible College graduate with a Baptist background. These men operate to some extent independently of one another, but their basic teaching and outlook are broadly the same. They work together in what they term 'covenanted relationships'. The Bradford house church movement is in the process of moving its headquarters to the Midlands, and in future there will be several different venues for its annual gathering which was originally known as 'Dales' Week.

There are distinct similarities in the outlook of those in this group with members of the 'Honor Oak Fellowship'. The founder and leader of this movement was a former Baptist minister, the late T Austin Sparks. He claimed to have received a divine revelation concerning the true nature of the Christian church as the body of Christ. This led him to assert that Christians should separate from the church order of which they had hitherto formed a part. The Honor Oak Fellowship in its day displayed a similar type of élitism to that which we find today in some charismatic groups. The quest in both cases was for the perfect church. Some have claimed that there are similarities between such teaching and that of the Chinese Christian Watchman Nee.

In the south of England there is a group of house churches loosely linked together under the name 'New Frontiers'. These churches recognise Terry Virgo as the leader of their 'apostolic team', and they gather for a convention each summer at 'The Downs' in Sussex.

Another wing of the house church movement is associated with the name of Gerald Coates who resides in Cobham, Surrey. Leaders sympathetic with this group, such as John Noble, David Tomlinson, Maurice Smith and Graham Perrins, are men who have enjoyed a longstanding personal friendship with Gerald Coates. They are probably the least organised of the house church groups, and display a good deal of flexibility.

They are also the most ready to co-operate with other Bible-believing Christians. They emphasise the prophetic ministry and have a real concern for evangelism.

The leader of yet another group is a Pastor George ('Wally') North, a group that is sometimes humorously referred to as the 'North Circular'. North has adopted Wesley's view on holiness and perfectionism, and uses the term 'new birth' for what others would refer to as 'baptism in the Spirit'. As a whole, groups linked with Pastor North tend to keep themselves to themselves and rarely join in fellowship with other Christians.

There is another group based on a small community in South Chard in Somerset. Here the disciplinary element is particularly strong, and emphasis is placed on the ministries of deliverance and healing. Men such as Harry Greenwood, Sid Purse and Ian Andrews are linked with this group. Chard has been associated with the practice of rebaptism on the basis that in the Acts of the Apostles baptism was always in the name of Jesus and this is therefore, in their opinion, the correct way to carry out Christ's command to baptise. Thus, people aready baptised as believers with the trinitarian formula have been encouraged to be rebaptised 'in the name of Jesus'. The South Chard fellowships, as well as those linked with Pastor North, were in existence before the house church movement as we know it today got under way.

In addition to the identifiable groups which we have mentioned, there are countless other Pentecostal fellowships which would claim to be entirely independent and autonomous. Some are known as 'New Community Churches', others are called 'King's Churches' or 'New Covenant Churches'. A very virile group is the Ichthus Fellowship, associated with Roger and Faith Forster. The Ichthus Fellowship is based in South-East London, and it is very much involved in church planting. Its ethos is Open Brethren, but it gives greater place to women's ministry than is customary either in Restorationist or Brethren circles.

The leaders in the various branches of 'Restorationism' are

one in thinking that denominations are not in the plan of God. They long to see the church following a New Testament pattern, with Christians living in a kingdom run according to God's order. They foresee an outpouring of God's Spirit as a prelude to the establishment of a kingdom, ready for the return of the King.

As well as the different groups we have mentioned, a number of charismatic communities have come into being in recent years. One such community is the Bethany Fellowship in Sussex, associated with Colin Urquhart, Bob Gordon, Michael Barling and others.

A community of a rather different order is the Bugbrooke Community in Northamptonshire. It is based on the local Baptist church and presided over by the pastor, Noel Stanton, and his fellow elders. The community provides a base for people who find it difficult to cope with life in the outside world. It began in a small way in 1973, but it has grown to the extent that over 500 people now live there. A trust exists which manages the various houses and businesses owned by the community. They work on the basis of a common purse and common ownership. Those joining hand over their possessions and their money, although they are given the option of later withdrawing and being repaid should they wish.

Noel Stanton and his fellow elders exercise their authority through small shepherding groups, but the teaching of the leader is accepted without question. The leadership generally is authoritarian. Members must seek permission from their elders for almost anything they wish to do. Because members live in close community, single people may not become friendly with a member of the opposite sex without first getting the elder's permission. Everything possible is done to eliminate the intrusion of 'the flesh'. Women are discouraged from dressing in a way that might draw attention to themselves. Competitive games of any kind are forbidden. No radios, television or pop music are allowed. The aim of the fellowship is to create a genuine reflection of the kingdom of God through what is known as the New Creation Community.

Sadly, the fellowship tends to become somewhat isolationist, élitist and remote from other Christian groups.

In the 1970s a number of Christian communities came into being. In 1971 Whatcome House was opened as the centre for the Barnabas Fellowship. The Rev and Mrs Reg East resigned from the livings of East and West Mersea in Essex, and moved to a Georgian mansion near Blandford in Dorset which they renovated in order to accommodate a community of ten and about thirty guests. They were anxious to welcome any who were open to the will of God and who were wanting to experience the power of the Spirit in their lives. Other communities were located at Post Green in Dorset, Lamplugh House in Yorkshire, Blaithwaite House in Cumbria, and Fellowship House in Brentwood. The German evangelical community, known as the Sisterhood of Mary, established a branch at Radlett in Hertfordshire. The Sisters of Mary soon created a deep impression on British Christians because of their transparent Christlikeness.

In the house church movement 'baptism in the Holy Spirit' is presented as being a spiritual experience subsequent to conversion and normally authenticated by speaking in tongues. Although it is conceded that in theory regeneration and enduement with power may occur simultaneously, it is argued that this is rarely the case in practice. Baptism in the Holy Spirit provides power in witness, effectiveness in prayer and, above all, an entrance into the realm of spiritual gifts. Most house church members would concede that baptism in the Spirit does not solve all problems and does not come to all in precisely the same way, although it usually follows the laying-on of hands and is evidenced by 'speaking in tongues'.

Baptism by immersion subsequent to conversion is the normal practice in the house churches. Considerable stress is placed on this. Baptism in infancy is regarded as invalid.

The exercise of spiritual gifts within the fellowship is an integral part of worship in the house churches. Thus, speaking in tongues with interpretation, prophecy, words of knowledge and healing are all encouraged. Worship is 'open' and theoretically unstructured, although in many cases the form it is likely to take is clearly predictable. The opening part of the service will concentrate on 'worship' songs. The congregation may remain standing for a considerable period of time while chorus after chorus is sung, some of them many times over. Those present are encouraged to express themselves freely by raising their hands, dancing, rattling tambourines, clapping, or any other activity deemed appropriate. The time of worship may last an hour or even longer. Words of prophecy are also encouraged. There may follow a briefer period of intercession and of sharing, then finally, as time permits, the exposition of Scripture. A worship service may last from two to three hours.

The Lord's Supper, usually referred to as the 'breaking of bread' in house church circles, is a focal point of worship. In some fellowships it is celebrated weekly and always with a complete absence of formality.

Generous giving is a feature of house churches. No seat-to-seat offerings are taken, but members subscribe with great generosity to local needs and to helping fellow members who may be specially needy. Tithing is standard practice.

Probably the most striking feature of all about a house church is its atmosphere of love and fellowship. Only Christian names are used, members greet one another with a loving embrace, and the atmosphere is that of a closely knit family.

The centre of gravity of church life is found in the house group. Each group will consist of a dozen or so people led by a house group leader who, in turn, is supervised by one of the elders. It is stressed that there must be regular commitment to the group since the purpose is to build relationships in depth. In most cases the groups meet in different members' homes. A group meeting will normally include a time of worship, of Bible study, of sharing experiences and needs, of intercession and of social enjoyment. A house group meeting normally lasts at least two hours and is held either weekly or at fortnightly intervals.

Most house churches adopt a pyramidal form of church

government. At the base of the pyramid are the church members, then there are the house group leaders, above them the elders, and higher up still are the 'apostles' who are available for counsel. A house church does not normally have a constitution in the generally accepted sense, nor a book of church rules. Most do not have a formal list of members. The elders 'emerge' and are 'recognised' by the members. Voting has no part to play in the proceedings. Commitment classes are held for new converts and are considered a must.

The issue of authority and submission is one which has received considerable publicity. The house churches believe they have got the balance right, although some will admit that from time to time mistakes have been made and authority has been overplayed. In principle, everyone has someone else to whom they submit, children to parents, wives to husbands, church members to elders, elders to apostles, and apostles to apostles (sometimes). There are considerable differences in churches as to the manner that submission is understood. Stories about church members seeking the permission of the elders to go on holiday are usually apocryphal! Teaching on submission is an integral part of the commitment course which members of house churches are asked to attend. Critics of the house churches suggest the movement is strongly coloured by male chauvinism! The leadership at all levels is usually in male hands.

The house churches are not cluttered up with a plethora of ancillary activities. Some do hold separate classes for children, but there are no specific organisations catering for different interests or age groups.

Each house group tends to see itself as the New Testament church in that particular neighbourhood, and so we have names such as the Chichester Christian Fellowship and the Southampton Community Church, which give the impression that they represent the sum total of Christian life and activity in that particular city.

It is interesting to note how the house church movement generally has developed a jargon of its own. Its members claim to be 'going God's way', or 'moving on in the things of the Spirit'. Stress is laid on 'body life' expressed through 'agape relationships'. House groups are often referred to as 'home cells', and some churches are designated 'new covenant communities'. The word 'restoration' sums up the vision that many have for their role in the history of the church. Other words that are frequently heard are: discipleship, commitment, covering, shepherding and submission. We also hear of people being 'slain in the Spirit', which presumably is synonymous with 'brokenness' but is expressed by literally falling to the ground as though in a trance. This frequently happens at healing services.

Christians generally are conscious that something unusual has been going on in the church, but many do not know how to assess it. There are those who write off the movement as a kind of spiritual aberration, devoid of any lasting significance. Some would go so far as to say it is, at least in part, carnal, fleshly, and to some degree even satanic. Others see it as the answer to the prayers of Christians who have zealously prayed for spiritual revival for years, regarding it as first and foremost a movement of God's Spirit.

Congregations in churches influenced by the movement are largely made up of a similar age group – those in their twenties and thirties. Among young people there seems to be increasing disillusionment with institutional religion in whatever form it may take. One is aware at the same time that the so-called freedom enjoyed in charismatic worship, for example, is itself in danger of becoming stereotyped. Today's revolution all too often becomes tomorrow's conformity.

Our God-given responsibility is to 'test the spirits' whether they are of God. One is tempted to say of the renewal movement within the historic denominations and of the house churches that, like the proverbial curate's egg, they are 'good in parts'. There are obvious dangers to which reference has already been made, such as divisiveness, élitism, authoritarianism and exclusivism. Nevertheless, there is a great deal that is clearly of God. The church needed to be reminded that it is meant to be a fellowship and not merely an institution – that it consists of all true believers, each of whom has a God-given ministry to perform. We needed to be reminded that the gifts of the Spirit were given to be used, and that they did not cease to be operative at the conclusion of the apostolic age. Congregational participation in worship is a scriptural principle if 1 Corinthians chapter 14 is to be taken seriously. The concept of a one-man ministry is rightly being questioned, and the need for an eldership is being stressed. All such moves are very much on the credit side.

It is said that when God does a new thing for us, we find it so difficult to keep a sense of balance. We should acknowledge that the restoration movement represents part of what God is doing in the world today, but it is not the only significant thing. The church needed to have the sort of jolt which the movement has provided. All too many churches have become 'institutionalised museums of respectable tradition instead of mobile ambulances driven by God's ever-moving Spirit'. A younger generation of Christians has found traditional church structures too restrictive for the kind of fellowship and worship they are seeking. Leaders in the house churches are ready to admit mistakes have been made. The charge of being schismatic may be true in some cases, but more often than not it is more a question of new wine not being able to exist in the old wineskins. Inevitably leaders tend to be individualists and often extremists. Such a charge, as we have seen, could have been levelled at John Wesley or William Booth. In spite of its shortcomings, many in different branches of the Christian church sincerely thank God for the impact of the whole charismatic movement and earnestly seek to conserve the wheat while brushing aside the chaff. It seems clear that within the past two or three decades, there has been a fresh outpouring of the Holy Spirit which has crossed denominational barriers and brought a new dimension of spiritual life to many Christians. Of course there are dangers – as Jonathan Edwards wrote: 'A work of God without stumbling blocks is never to be expected.' Inevitably, such a movement attracts both cranks and charlatans. John Wesley suffered many heartaches because of the foolish antics of some of his followers. Having faced the dangers, we must avoid throwing away the baby with the bath-water.

The renewal movement has created both a new unity among Christians and also new divisions. It is always sad when a movement which is clearly of God is manipulated by man. The number of splits in evangelical churches in recent years is legion, but the fact remains that historically renewal movements have always tended to spawn new groupings – this was so with the Reformation and the evangelical revival. George Tarleton, one of the early leaders, asserts that 'the house church movement is dead'. He means, of course, the formative period is over. So-called 'house churches' have in many cases outgrown houses and meet in schools and public halls. At the same time some of the larger denominational churches are splitting up into smaller fellowship groups and meeting less frequently for corporate worship. We must wait with patience to see how the future patterns will develop.

Within the charismatic movement there are two clearly discernible groups which for convenience could be named the renewalists and the restorationists. The renewalists, generally speaking, look for change within the framework of their own denomination, whereas the restorationists believe that 'anything that promotes denominationalism, either individually or corporately, is sin and needs to be clearly labelled as such'. That basically is the standpoint of the house churches. Thus we are faced with the 'stay in' or 'come out' dilemma. David Watson was one who believed that Christians should pray for true spiritual renewal within existing church structures, while Arthur Wallis sees the house churches as the new wineskins to contain the new wine. He sees no future in denominations as such. Incidentally, Arthur Torrey, a grandson of the American evangelist, R A Torrey, has pointed out that every great revival movement has spawned various groups which have sought to restore the church to the New Testament pattern. He found that in America alone at least sixty new denominations came into being as the result of nineteenth and twentieth century revivals, all purporting to restore the church on truly New Testament lines.

In her book *Something's Happening* Eileen Vincent writes very disparagingly of those who stop short by seeking only renewal and not embracing teaching on restoration: 'Renewal is a limited view of restoration which seeks to contain the work of the Spirit within the bounds and understanding of a given denominational tradition. Obviously that restricts the restoring activity of the Spirit.' She maintains that 'to only work for renewal is to fall short of the purpose of God.' In point of fact, there are at least three main bodies of Pentecostalists – those in the Pentecostal denominations, those who are to be found in the house churches, and those existing as distinct groups within the mainline denominations. When we examine the house church movement we soon discover that there are different groups which do not see eye to eye with one another, representing different emphases within the movement itself.

There are striking similarities between the beginnings of the house church movement and the early days of the Christian Brethren. Both movements began within the Church of England and had no intention originally of becoming separate denominations. Both movements were a protest against clericalism and institutional religion. A wing of the Brethren movement became increasingly exclusivist and autocratic, while others endeavoured to maintain fellowship with other Christians across denominational boundaries. A similar development would appear to be taking place within the charismatic movement at the present time – a section see themselves as the true church and call on Christians from the various denominations to join their ranks, while another section emphasises renewal and rejoices to see it wherever it may be found.

Eileen Vincent justifies in this way those who leave their local church and form a house church: 'If the local church is restrictive and set in unyielding traditional ways, those within the body of Christ who are growing, expanding, developing and changing will shed their old allegiances like a butterfly emerging from a spent pupa case.' She argues that a Christian is only entitled to worship in his or her local church if it is a living organism, and by that she means 'it moves in the power of the Spirit and seeks restoration'.

For some with a traditional church background there are hurdles to overcome. There is, for example, the thorny question of baptism. The house churches stand solidly for believers' baptism by total immersion. Eileen Vincent argues: 'The restoration of all things demands a purist view. Baptism is a foundational doctrine of the church and must be returned to its rightful importance if we are to see the full blessing of the restoration of all things.' Needless to say, those in the house churches would have no qualms about baptising those who were 'christened' in infancy. For them believers' baptism is a matter of basic principle and is the only valid form of baptism.

Those in the house churches freely admit that many denominational churches have experienced renewal expressed in greater liberty in praise and worship and the recognition of the place of spiritual gifts, but they feel that true 'restoration' demands a fresh start – it cannot be contained within the bounds of existing denominational structures. One is tempted to point out that in other spheres restoration does not suggest erecting a new building but working on an existing structure in order to restore it to its former glory.

The house church movement has been severely criticised because of its emphasis on leadership and discipline. Those in the movement would argue in defence that the church needs leaders who really lead and who do not apologise for the authority God has given them.

It is difficult to predict the future as far as the house church movement is concerned. Some will undoubtedly continue to go to extremes and will be 'out on a limb' as far as mainline Christianity is concerned. It is likely that Anglican churches which have experienced renewal will remain in the Church of England fold, but some free churches may sever their links with their denominations. It would be a tragedy if this movement, which many of us believe is of God, were allowed either to fizzle out or to become sectarian. The danger of this happening can be averted if the leadership of dominant personalities can be circumvented and the tendency towards regimentation overcome.

The pipe-dream of a perfect church has captivated men and women before now, but history has shown that no such church will exist until Christ comes again. Meanwhile, we would do well to absorb the valuable lessons the house churches have taught us, recognising that institutional religion is no substitute for vital Christianity.

15

Why All These Denominations?

In earlier chapters I have tried to cover most, if not all of the different denominations to be found in Britain today. The picture presented is a complex one, and for those who have newly entered the Christian fold it must create many problems. Some tend to dismiss the whole subject lightly, paying scant regard to history and oversimplifying the situation as a result. Others, holding tenaciously to their denominational emphases, have little interest or concern for those outside their own particular group. It would be true to say, however, that, generally speaking, denominational barriers are lower today than ever before, and there is more interdenominational collaboration than previous generations ever knew. An increasing number of young Christians, especially those in the house churches, regard denominations as a major hindrance in spreading the gospel.

At the official level, of course, there is a close link between the larger denominations. The British Council of Churches, which is the national expression of the World Council of Churches, links together both Anglican and free churches. The Free Church Federal Council, as its name implies, provides a link between the leading nonconformist bodies. The Evangelical Alliance draws together churches, societies and individual Christians of all denominations – both Church of England and nonconformist – who are at one in their adherence to the great biblical truths set out in its Basis of Faith, whether or not their particular denomination has formal links with the British Council of Churches. The British Evangelical Council seeks to draw together evangelical churches in Britain which have no ties whatever with the British Council of Churches. They include in their membership the Free Church of Scotland, the Fellowship of Independent Evangelical Churches, the Evangelical Presbyterian Church of Northern Ireland, and some Grace Baptist groups.

There is, then, a great deal being done unitedly in these days. At the local level there is often a council of churches. This normally brings together most, if not all, of the Protestant churches – Anglican and free. In many instances, but by no means in every case, the local council is affiliated to the British Council of Churches. The local Free Church Council, where such exists, unites the main denominational nonconformist churches. The effectiveness of these bodies depends to a large degree on the quality of their local leadership. Generally speaking, they are responsible for arranging united services, Christian Aid Week, pulpit exchanges and other such activities.

In addition to the groupings already mentioned there are in some of the larger towns evangelical fellowships which bring together those Christians who could be described as 'conservative evangelicals' (that is, evangelicals who accept the full inspiration of the Scriptures). Many of them are affiliated to the Evangelical Alliance. Such fellowships arrange activities which particularly commend themselves to the evangelical section of the community, including conventions for the deepening of spiritual life, Bible rallies, united evangelistic campaigns, and the like. Here again, much depends on the quality of the leadership that is given.

As far as local clergy and ministers are concerned, they have, in most cases, opportunities for meeting together on a fairly informal basis at the interdenominational level in local fraternals.

It would probably be true to say that in these days there are often closer links across denominational barriers between those of a similar theological outlook than there are within any one denomination. Spiritual unity does not depend on church union. It can and does exist quite apart from that. It enables Christians of varying church traditions to work, to pray and to witness together when they are agreed upon the fundamentals of the faith.

One of the matters upon which Christians in general may differ, but upon which almost all evangelical Christians are agreed, is the nature of the church. A statement on this subject, for example, appeared as long ago as 1962 above the signatures of nearly forty different evangelical leaders drawn from the ranks of the Church of England, the Church of Scotland, Methodists, Congregationalists, Baptists, the Fellowship of Independent Evangelical Churches, Pentecostalists and the Christian Brethren. The statement was as follows:

The Church of God consists of His elect of every land and every age, who have been united to Christ by His grace through faith, and are indwelt by the Holy Spirit. This union with Christ, signified by baptism though not created by it, finds visible expression when believers meet together for worship and the ministry of the Word, and at the Lord's Table.

This spiritual unity is further expressed when Christians of varying traditions participate together in the Lord's Supper, unhindered by differences on secondary matters. The existence of this God-given unity does not, however, absolve Christians from endeavouring to understand the differing viewpoints held on these secondary matters, such as forms of worship, systems of government, and orders of ministry.

Nevertheless, there are certain essential doctrines on which no compromise is possible, such as the Trinity of Father, Son and Holy Spirit; the deity of Christ; the sole sufficiency of His atoning work for the salvation of men; the supreme authority of Holy Scripture in all matters of faith and practice; the justification of the sinner by the grace of God through faith alone; and the priesthood of the whole Church whereby every believer has direct access to God the Father through the one Mediator, Jesus Christ. To the extent to which churches (whether in membership of the

World Council of Churches or not) fail to express these truths, to that extent they fall short of being churches in the New Testament sense, though individuals within them may be true believers.

The different denominations have much to learn from and to teach one another. Each of them bears witness to some particular aspect of Bible truth, and their collective witness is greater than that of any one group. Since our temperaments vary so greatly it is hardly surprising that we express ourselves somewhat differently in our modes of worship. The ordered form of a liturgical service appeals to some, while others are drawn to the more boisterous enthusiasm of the Salvation Army or the house churches. Some are helped by the simplicity of the free church service, while others shrink from any semblance of an 'ordered' service at all and prefer to wait upon God in quietness, speaking, praying or singing only as they feel led by the Spirit.

The fact that these divisions do exist does not discredit the Christian faith, nor does it mean that Christian people are at variance over fundamental doctrines. The plain fact is that the New Testament does not lay down hard and fast rules over such matters as church government or the Christian ministry. Over these issues there was and must still be a measure of elasticity. Where, however, there is common consent to the fact that the Bible, as originally given, is the very word of God and our supreme and final authority in all matters of faith and conduct, then there is remarkable spiritual unity and a readiness to co-operate in many different ways. One thing we can say is that far from constituting an excuse for people to remain outside the church, the existence of these various denominations presents the opportunity for every one of us to find a spiritual home where we feel most happy.

There are those who look forward to the day when there may be one evangelical church, bringing together all evangelicals out of the different denominations. In theory this may be very fine, but experience would suggest that it is hardly likely to be a practical proposition. The strength, as well as the weakness, of evangelicals has so often been in their individualism. One seriously questions how long they would remain united in one all-embracing denomination. It is better, surely, to recognise differences on such secondary matters as modes of worship and systems of church government, and at the same time acknowledge basic unity in essential matters of faith, being willing to co-operate on the basis of that unity to the greatest possible extent whenever opportunity offers. Our so-called 'unhappy divisions' need not be so unhappy if only we can see them in the right light.

One has to admit to mixed feelings in assessing the overall picture of the church in Britain today. It is computed that considerably less than ten per cent of the population regularly attend any place of worship, whether Protestant or Roman Catholic. Unquestionably in industrial areas the percentage is far lower. Furthermore, in most congregations the numerical predominance of women over men is most noticeable. It is no uncommon sight to see church buildings that have been sold and are now being used for commercial purposes. In rural areas there are very many local chapels where the regular congregation musters less than a dozen in all. On the other hand, there are churches, particularly in some of the more prosperous suburban areas, which are filled to capacity. This in itself is a feature of modern church life. It is on the whole the so-called 'middle class' section of the community that goes to church, whereas in the more thickly populated areas the numbers of those who regularly attend a place of worship are lamentably small. Even the Salvation Army no longer finds it easy to make contact with that section of the community which it was primarily founded to reach.

Material prosperity has in general led to spiritual apathy; no one denomination can claim to have found the answer to the prevailing indifference. Some have been more successful than others in meeting the challenge of these days, but wherever one looks the need is the same – the need of spiritual awakening. Someone has described the era preceding the evangelical revival as being one of dim ideals and expiring hopes – an age of materialism. This might also be a fitting description of our own day. It is the prayer of all thoughtful Christians that this challenging situation may lead to a spiritual awakening such as was associated with the illustrious names of John and Charles Wesley and George Whitefield in the eighteenth century.

Perhaps one of the encouraging features of the present time is that more and more people are becoming conscious of their country's spiritual need, as well as of their own personal need, and they are beginning to pray for something to happen. Indeed it could be said that something has happened. We may yet wait for a heaven-sent revival but we have witnessed renewal coming to many congregations. Opinions may be sharply divided over the charismatic movement, but few would deny that there has been a work of the Spirit in our midst. As a result of this, we have a spate of 'house churches' not linked with any particular denomination but exercising the gifts of the Spirit and engaging in free and spontaneous worship. Young people in particular have been drawn into these groups which look for their leadership to different men, most of whom would be regarded as modern-day 'apostles'. While it is true that to some extent the membership of these churches is made up of disgruntled members of different denominations, that is not the whole story. These churches have come to stay and are being strengthened by a steady stream of converts, many of whom have no church background whatsoever.

One thing is certain: today's Christians, particularly the younger ones, are looking for churches that are truly alive, and they have little interest in the bureaucracy which for too long has had a stranglehold on church life.

16

On the Fringe and Beyond – Some Christian Deviations

In a book about the church in Britain it may seem out of place to include a chapter on 'isms' and 'ologies' – cults that are distinct from traditional Christianity. We shall not concern ourselves with those cults which make no pretence of being Christian and which in some cases have closer affinities with the mystic religions of the Orient. There are, however, a number of groups who at least pay lip service to the authority of Scripture, even though in some cases their interpretation of Scripture would appear to be decidedly fanciful.

Seventh-Day Adventists

We start by looking at what is probably the denomination which is closest of all to orthodox Christianity. The Adventists claim they are concerned simply to uphold 'the great fundamentals of Bible truth'. In many respects they do in fact do this. The main point of divergence between them and the Christian church generally relates to their insistence that we should observe Saturday – the Jewish Sabbath – as our day of worship rather than Sunday. They believe strongly in the Lord's return and in the past have made the mistake of date-fixing. Adventists have strong views on a number of issues – tithing of one's income is obligatory, and abstinence from alcohol, tobacco and narcotics is regarded as a Christian duty. They have a splendid reputation for their medical and relief work, and good citizenship is encouraged in home, school and church. To quote from an Adventist leaflet: 'Organised in 1863, and basing its faith wholly on the Bible, it set out on its world task to reillumine truths tarnished or forgotten during Christianity's long and tortuous history, and to bring them into focus as God's message of hope for these momentous times.'

Evangelical Christians have been divided over the attitude they should adopt towards the Adventist Church. Some gladly work with them, while others feel they take a legalistic stand and are divisive because of their insistence on Sabbath observance. There are about 16,000 active members of the Seventh-Day Adventist Church in Britain, and probably between one and two million in the world.

Jehovah's Witnesses

The Jehovah's Witnesses claim to accept the authority of Scripture yet they deny some of the fundamental teachings of the Bible. Of all the cults they are the most active and the most aggressive. Their founder was Charge Taze Russell, a compelling speaker and brilliant organiser, but highly critical of orthodox Christianity. In 1884 he launched 'Zion's Watch Tower Society'. The name 'Jehovah's Witness' was not used until 1931, some years after Russell's death.

Jehovah's Witnesses perpetuate a heresy which was condemned in the fourth century when put forth by Arius, a presbyter of Alexandria. For them, Jesus was a created being and only God 'in a secondary sense'. They repudiate utterly the doctrine of the Trinity, and like some other cults they have indulged in date-fixing in relation to the second coming of Christ. They are adept at twisting Scripture for their own ends and make no secret of the fact that they hate all organised religion. Nevertheless, they constitute a challenge to the Christian church through their zeal in propagating what they believe, and through their giving. There are probably about 90,000 Jehovah's Witnesses in Britain, and every one of them is regarded as a worker for the cause. Their meeting places are called 'Kingdom Halls'.

The Mormon Church

Similar in size and influence come the Mormons, or the Church of Jesus Christ of Latter-Day Saints as they prefer to be called. There may be as many as 100,000 adherents to this cult in Britain, and the church has an ambitious building programme. Founded by Joseph Smith, Mormonism is based largely on the Book of Mormon which purports to give the history of the ancient inhabitants of America. The genuineness of the claims made for this book is open to serious question. Mormons claim that the Book of Mormon in its original form was completed around 400 AD, yet large sections of the Authorised Version of the Bible (published in 1611) are found in it. Although Mormons use orthodox terminology, their views are far from orthodox. They are totally opposed to the Christian concept of a triune God. They see God as a physical being – 'God himself was once as we are now, and is an exalted man'. Christ is not seen as the unique Son of God, and the Holy Spirit is said to work only in those who have been baptised as Mormons and have received the laying-on of hands by the Mormon priesthood.

Baptism is regarded as all-important and for that reason Mormons believe in 'baptism for the dead'. Living Mormons are encouraged to be baptised vicariously for their dead relatives so that they too may be given a chance to be saved. Mormons also believe in 'celestial marriage'. This takes place in a Mormon Temple and ensures the continuance of the marriage after death.

Basically Mormons hold the view they have been raised up in these 'latter days' to restore true Christianity on earth. Joseph Smith, for them, was a divinely inspired prophet who supplemented the preaching of Christ by revealing further truth.

Christadelphians

From time to time one sees placards inviting the public to attend a series of Bible lectures, often related to prophecy. In all probability these are being sponsored by the Christadelphians, a sect founded by Dr John Thomas in the early nineteenth century. He emigrated to America in 1832, but revisited England on several occasions, founding several churches of which the dominant one was in Birmingham. The most influential British leader was Robert Roberts who wrote the book *Christendom Astray from the Bible*.

Although loud in their protestations of adherence to the Scriptures, Christadelphians reject the notion of judgement to come, the doctrine of the Trinity and the atoning nature of Christ's death. Salvation is through persistence in good works, baptism and acceptance of Christadelphian teaching. Each ecclesia (church) is independent without an ordained ministry. There are nearly 20,000 Christadelphians in the British Isles. In some respects, their teaching has certain similarities with that of Jehovah's Witnesses.

The Family of Love

In the heady days of 'flower power' when the Jesus Movement flourished in California, a group came to these shores calling themselves the Children of God. At first they seemed to be keen Christians eager to live out the Christian life in simplicity and sincerity. As time went on, however, it became clear that the teaching followed by this group was not merely the teaching of the Bible, but was being supplemented by instruction from another quarter, their mysterious leader, David (alias 'Moses') Berg. Alongside the Scriptures members are expected to read regular letters and papers often referred to as Mo-letters, issued by Berg. Some of these are relatively harmless, but others contain teaching which is anti-Christian as well as being antisocial. There is strong denunciation of 'the system' – government, education and orthodox medicine, as well as the church. Members engage in 'flirty fishing' – recruiting by sexual seduction – offering sex as a means of showing the love of God. Those who join the movement submit to autocratic leadership and rigid discipline. They are asked to cut their ties with family and friends in order to join a 'Family of Love' commune. They see themelves as the only true Christians in the world. David Berg is said to be God's prophet for this century, bringing new truth to light and giving the only legitimate interpretation of Scripture.

'The Way'

'The Way' is the name of a professedly Christian group that has in fairly recent years established itself in the United Kingdom. Its founder was an American, Victor Paul Wierwille, who started off as a minister in the Evangelical and Reformed Church in 1941.

Wierwille believed he had been shown insights hidden since the time of the apostle Paul. He rejected the true deity of Jesus Christ and the personhood of the Holy Spirit, saying instead that the Holy Spirit is an impersonal power or ability. Speaking in tongues he saw to be the acceptable sign of true worship and the necessary indication that a person has been born again. Wierwille's theology is a blend of Unitarianism, dispensationalism and Pentecostalism.

Although 'The Way' appears orthodox, its followers preach a different gospel about a different Jesus. The preincarnate existence of Jesus is denied and for 'The Way' Jesus Christ is not God but a specially created perfect being whose body came from Mary and whose soul or life principle was specially created by God in Mary's womb. Wierwille repeats the heresy associated with Paul of Samosata in the third century and Arius in the fourth.

'The Way' consists of about 60 or more communities with

about 1,500 people involved altogether.

Worldwide Church of God

Most of us have come across a glossy magazine called *The Plain Truth* which is offered freely on station bookstalls. Many of its articles are very readable and we may well wonder about the source from which it emanates. The answer is Herbert W Armstrong of the Worldwide Church of God. Like so many others in the cults, Armstrong and his followers believe that they and they alone have the truth and that every Christian denomination and every other sect is in error.

Armstrong accepts the totally unproven theory that the ten 'lost' tribes when the Assyrians conquered Israel are today to be identified with the Anglo-Saxon peoples of Britain and America. Armstrong rejects the doctrine of a triune God – Father, Son and Holy Spirit – although he affirms belief in Christ's deity. However, his death on the cross did not achieve man's salvation but gave everyone the opportunity of a fresh start. We are now free to earn our salvation by obeying God's commandments. The true church is made up of those who accept Armstrong's teaching. The observance of the Jewish Sabbath is legally binding on all Christians.

The teaching of Herbert Armstrong has affinities with that of Jehovah's Witnesses, Mormons and Christadelphians.

Christian Science

Most of us will have come across a Christian Science reading room, and in the window we may well see a copy of the Bible with another book alongside it, *Science and Health with the Key to the Scriptures*, published originally in 1875.

Mary Baker Eddy was the founder of Christian Science for which she made great claims. 'The second appearing of Jesus is unquestionably the spiritual advent of the advancing idea of God as in Christian Science,' she wrote. She also claimed: 'It is undoubtedly true that Christian Science is destined to become the one and only religion on this planet.'

Christian Science has been defined as a system of healing based upon the old philosophical concept of the non-existence of matter. Its leading principle is that there is nothing material in the universe; matter does not exist. 'Mind is all; matter is nought.' Mankind is said to be under the tyranny of the mortal mind. Christian Science is, in fact, a modern form of Gnosticism – it has much in common with Theosophy and Buddhism, while employing the terminology of Christianity.

There are probably 13,000 Christian Scientists in Britain drawn almost entirely from the middle and upper classes of society. In a fallen world like ours it is hard to understand how people can be led to believe that sin and sickness are other than real. Moreover, our Lord's death is evidence that he took sin so seriously he was prepared to die in order to procure man's forgiveness.

Spiritualism

In view of Scripture's clear-cut condemnation of dabbling with the occult and seeking to communicate with the dead, it is somewhat surprising to come across churches which are designated as 'Christian Spiritualist'. In point of fact, those spiritualists who claim Christian connections have a very different understanding of the Christian faith from that commonly held by Bible-believing Christians. They stress the universal fatherhood of God and brotherhood of man but have little understanding of the atoning work of Christ on the cross.

Unitarianism

There are in different parts of the country Unitarian or Free Christian churches. These hold to a system of thought which rejects the notion of a triune God and the deity of Christ. Unitarians believe (some of us would feel rather naïvely) in the essential goodness of man, and they resolutely oppose any kind of credal test which would limit the spirit of enquiry.

They reject teaching regarding the Fall, the need for atonement, and the fact of eternal damnation. English Unitarianism may be traced back to John Biddle, who was imprisoned for his Unitarian beliefs. Essex Chapel in London was founded in 1774, and soon there were Unitarian congregations in Leeds and Birmingham. Many have, of course, held Unitarian views without necessarily attending a Unitarian church. Modern Unitarians stress the teaching of the Sermon on the Mount and the universal fatherhood of God and brotherhood of man. They follow a congregational pattern of church government. They number just over 7,000 members.

The New Church

The Church of the New Jerusalem, or simply 'New Church', owes its origin to Emmanuel Swedenborg, although he himself made no effort to gather followers to himself. His writings, mostly in Latin, were translated into English. It fell to a Methodist, Robert Hindmarsh, to organise those who were influenced by them. Ministers were ordained, and by 1789, the first general conference was held at Great Eastcheap in London. Worship meetings of the New Church tend to be liturgical, with preaching based on what are considered to be the 'inspired' parts of the Bible – twenty-nine books of the Old Testament and five in the New Testament. Baptism and the

Lord's Supper are observed. Membership in Britain is about 4,500 in all.

Swedenborg's views were decidedly unorthodox. To him God was an infinite man existing in a perfect human form. He flatly denied the existence of the Trinity, claiming that at the incarnation, the One God was born of Mary, and 'derived hereditary evil' from her, although he 'had no actual evil or evil that was his own'. As John Wesley pointed out, Swedenborg revived an ancient heresy, that of the Sabellians and Patripassians.

To Swedenborg, the cross was not an atoning sacrifice, but a 'subjugation of the powers of evil'. He strongly denied the scriptural doctrine of 'justification by faith alone'.

Swedenborg declared that there would be no future resurrection or judgement since he had been permitted to see the Last Judgement in the world of spirits in 1757. That year ushered in a new dispensation, and this was marked by the formation of the New (Jerusalem) Church.

A man of enquiring mind and great intellect, and essentially a scientist, Swedenborg in middle life became the subject of strange dreams and visions. He believed that by this means he had been brought into touch with the spirit world and had visited both heaven and hell. Swedenborg gave up his scientific career and concentrated on writing down his religious ideas. John Wesley, who was his contemporary, described Swedenborg as 'one of the most ingenious, lively, entertaining madmen that ever set pen to paper'. He saw Swedenborg's works as being 'dreams of a disordered imagination'.

The Unification Church

Popularly known as Moonies, the followers of Dr Sun Myung Moon adopted the name Unification Church in 1975. The sect claims to be aiming at the unification of worldwide Christianity. Dr Moon says he was divinely commissioned 'to restore God's perfect kingdom on earth'. His book *Divine Principles* has been described as a mixture of oriental philosophy, Christian terminology and offbeat scriptural interpretations. For the 'Moonies' their founder is Lord of the Second Advent, the new Messiah, the true parent of mankind. Basic Christian doctrines are twisted beyond recognition. Cult members are taught that the outside world is in the grip of Satan and the only safe, reliable place on earth is within the Moon family. They are encouraged to sever their links with their own families.

As one looks at these different deviations from traditional Christianity – and I have only mentioned a few – certain traits are discernible. In many cases there is a failure to acknowledge the full deity of our Lord and to understand the meaning of his death on the cross. Behind most cults is a 'charismatic' leader claiming to have had a special revelation from God which supplements the teaching of Scripture, and demanding absolute and unquestioning obedience from his followers. In some cases this means severe curtailment of meaningful communication with family and friends. Solomon declared that there is nothing new under the sun, and it is a fact that in many cases we have ancient heresies in modern dress.

In these days when institutional religion is discounted, the field is open for those who wish to propagate teaching which is different from that with which people in general may be vaguely familiar. Furthermore, in a permissive society, some form of backlash is inevitable. Hence the fact that there are those who welcome authoritarianism and are prepared to hand over the control of their lives to others.

It is important to differentiate between a deviation and a heresy. In the main the latter springs from a misunderstanding of the person and work of Christ. There is much truth in the couplet,

> 'What think ye of Christ?' is the test
> To try both your state and your scheme;
> You cannot be right in the rest
> Unless you think rightly of him.

According to Webster's dictionary a heresy is 'a doctrine or opinion that is contrary to the fundamental doctrine or creed of any particular church'. The word 'cult' basically describes 'a system of religious worship', but it has come to be associated largely with teaching which is heterodox and with systems which owe their origin to the particular leader, usually of an authoritarian disposition. 'Deviation' suggests teaching which accepts basic Christian concepts but may over-emphasise or distort one or more truths, upsetting the balance of the faith. We have been warned in Scripture to expect a multitude of 'false Christs' and 'false prophets' in the latter days, and this is happening before our very eyes.

Further Reading

J Bax, *The Good Wine* (Church House Publishing)
M C Burrell, *The Challenge of the Cults* (IVP)
Burrell and Wright, *Some Modern Faiths* (IVP)
D Coffey, *Build that Bridge* (Kingsway)
J Coutts, *The Salvationists* (Mowbrays)
R E Davies, *Methodism* (Epworth)
Evangelical and Congregational (Evangelical Fellowship of
    Congregational Churches)
J Graham, *The Giant Awakes* (Marshall Pickering)
W Hollenweger, *The Pentecostals* (SCM)
D Jackman, *Understanding the Church* (Kingsway)
Gavin Reid (editor), *Hope for the Church of England?*
    (Kingsway)
H H Rowdon, *The Origins of the Brethren* (Pickering &
Inglis)
M Sorrell, *The Peculiar People* (Paternoster)
E Vincent, *Something's Happening* (Marshall Pickering)
T Virgo, *Restoration in the Church* (Kingsway)
A Walker, *Restoring the Kingdom* (Hodder & Stoughton)